# *Eyewitness to*

# GETTYSBURG

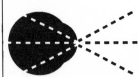

This Large Print Book carries the
Seal of Approval of N.A.V.H.

# Eyewitness to GETTYSBURG

The story of Gettysburg as told by the leading correspondent of his day.

*With an introduction and notes by John W. Schildt*

**G.K. Hall & Co. • Thorndike, Maine**

Published in 2000 by arrangement with White Mane Publishing Company, Inc.
Maps are from Charles Carleton Coffin, *Marching to Victory* (New York: Harper and Brothers, 1889), pp. 160–282.

G.K. Hall Large Print American History Series.

The text of this Large Print edition is unabridged.
Other aspects of the book may vary from the original edition.

Set in 16 pt. Plantin by Warren S. Doersam.

Printed in the United States on permanent paper.

**Library of Congress Cataloging-in-Publication Data**

Coffin, Charles Carleton, 1823–1896.
    [Marching to victory.  Chapter 9–13]
    Eyewitness to Gettysburg : the story of Gettysburg as told by the leading correspondent of his day / with an introduction and notes by John W. Schildt.
       p.  cm.
  Originally published: Marching to victory, chapters 9–13.
 New York : Harper & Brothers, 1889.
  Includes bibliographical references. (p. 210)
  ISBN 0-7838-9088-5 (lg. print : hc : alk. paper)
  1. Gettysburg (Pa.), Battle of, 1863 — Personal narratives.
2. Coffin, Charles Carleton, 1823–1896.  I. Schildt, John W.
II. Title.
E475.53 .C74  2000
973.7′349—dc21                              00-039632

# Table of Contents

# Introduction

## *The Man —*
## *Charles Carleton Coffin*

*Most Americans* are unfamiliar with the name of Charles Carleton Coffin. Yet he was a great American war correspondent, the Ernie Pyle of his era. He related well with officers and men, as well as the civilians in the path of the armies. Little had been written of Coffin. However, his biographer, W. E. Griffin, states that Coffin was "a soldier of the pen and knight of the truth."

Coffin was tall and well built. He had sparkling blue eyes, and loved a joke. Even in his old age, "he was still a boy at heart."

Coffin came from the rugged backwoods of New Hampshire. Like most of the Coffin clan, Charles could trace his roots to Tristam Coffin who sailed from Plymouth, England to the colonies in 1642. The Coffins came originally from Alwington, England. In appreciation of his roots, Charles gave the name Alwington to his post-Civil War home.

The premier correspondent of the Civil War was born in Boscawen, New Hampshire on July

26, 1823. He was home schooled. His parents used the famed "New England Primer."

Life as a boy in rural New Hampshire was tough. Charles' clothing was homespun. His mother cooked and heated the house from the open fireplace. Brown bread, apples, pork and beans, pumpkin pies, etc. were the main dishes. Village life centered around the church. The house of worship was unheated, and folks shivered during winter services.

In 1841, Charles met the great statesman Daniel Webster. The politician spoke at the Merrimac County Fair. Webster spoke to the teenager about his fine yolk of oxen.

The following winter, Charles was ill. Curious about all subjects, he bought a book about surveying. The book made a profound impression on the youngster. He saw the beauty and order of the universe in mathematical principles governing surveys. It gave him an engineer's eye. From then on Charles had an interest in roads, rivers, fields, elevations, etc. This eye became invaluable in his future years as a correspondent. The reader will note his descriptions in his writing on Gettysburg.

In his late teens, Charles went to work in a lumbering operation. His labor helped him raise sixty dollars to purchase an organ for his church. Coffin became the first organist.

Coffin left Boscawen for the bustling city of Boston, then a city of 75,000. At age twenty-one, he wanted to explore the world. Soon, this self-taught man was hired as a surveyor for the Concord Road.

During the project, a nearby axeman lost control of his axe. The blade chopped deeply into Coffin's left ankle, inflicting a severe wound. The injury brought an end to the surveying work, and caused Coffin to be laid up. This severe injury prevented Coffin from seeing duty as a soldier in the Civil War.

On February 18, 1846, Coffin married Sally Russell Farmer. This was a childless union, yet a long and happy marriage of fifty years. Recovering from his ankle injury, Charles obtained a job in the engineering division of the Northern Railroad. He did lumbering work on the side. Soon he and Sally were able to purchase a farm in West Boscawen.

Coffin lacked a college education. However, he was a brilliant man. He was self taught in the fields of engineering and music, and lumbering. Then he became interested in the new field of electricity. He helped construct a power line from Boston to Cambridge. His father-in-law then asked him to construct a telegraph fire alarm. Apparently Coffin's work resulted in the first electronically transmitted fire alarm. After working on this project, Coffin felt burned out.

Coffin then made a major vocational change. He was employed by the Boston *Journal*. He writes:

I saw that what the public wanted was news

in condensed form; that the day for stately editorials was passing away; that short statements and arguments, which went like an arrow to the mark, were what the public would be likely to read. I formed my style of writing with that in view.

Always a student, Coffin studied the speeches of Daniel Webster and Edmund Burke and others. Their approach helped him formulate his style.

Meeting Daniel Webster, reading a book on surveying, employment with the Boston *Journal*, these were all milestones in the life of Charles C. Coffin. The summer of 1854 brought another milestone.

Charles and Sally visited the Saratoga battlefield. There his grandfather had fought in 1777. For the first time in his life, Charles was able to visit a battlefield, and in his mind reconstruct the scene of action. He even found a bullet which further enticed his interest in history.

Funds from his inventions brought additional income to the Coffins. This money enabled Charles to visit Washington, D.C. His impression was interesting. It seemed like an "overgrown village." He wrote:

Washington was a straggling city, thoroughly southern. There was not a decent hotel. The National was regarded as the best. Nearly all the public men were in boarding houses.

Coffin visited the U.S. Capitol. He admired the paintings in the rotunda. He went to the Senate gallery and was enthralled with the speeches of Thomas Hart Benton of Missouri, and Robert Toombs of Georgia.

Inheriting 80 acres of land in Illinois, Coffin traveled to that state to inspect the land. While in Illinois he visited Chicago and wrote about mud, knee deep in the streets.

Coffin attended the Republican National Convention in Chicago in 1860. He was surprised at the animosity between the delegates from New York and Pennsylvania. Each were seeking to gain votes for their favorite sons. He learned that many of the delegates were leaning toward a "western man." Coffin found Thurlow Weed of New York staring at a photograph of Abraham Lincoln, looking, "pale and excited."

Coffin was in the group that traveled from Chicago to Springfield to advise Lincoln that he had won the Republican nomination for the presidency. The Lincoln boys were on the fence in front of the house. Coffin was one of the writers covering the 1860 political campaign. One night as he ate his supper of cheese and crackers, he saw two hungry mice staring at him. He felt the nation was headed for a serious crisis.

Coffin was present in Washington on March 4, 1861, when Lincoln was inaugurated. He walked in the spring moonlight with Senator Henry Wilson from Massachusetts, a man who would become one of his best friends. In the moonlight, the unfinished dome of the U.S. Capitol loomed in front of the two men. The sight spoke to Coffin. He wondered if the dome would ever be finished. Senator Wilson stated that he believed war was coming, "but the people of this country will not give up the Union."

Long opposed to slavery and succession, there was no doubt as to Coffin's loyalty. But how could he serve. The cut from the axe had severely damaged his ankle. Therefore, military service was out of the question. Senator Wilson came to his aid, and acknowledging Coffin's eye for detail and way with words, advised him to become a correspondent and cover the action.

Charles Carleton Coffin took the advice, and the rest is history. Coffin visited the camps and fortifications around Washington. He interviewed generals and privates. He wrote human interest accounts. The Boston *Journal* was so impressed with Coffin's account of the Battle of Bull Run, that they hired him to cover the war at the great sum of twenty-five dollars per week. His instructions were "Keep the *Journal* at the front." He did not have any assistants, but many times he was the first to get details of an action to the media. His biographer says that Coffin was the only correspondent to serve throughout the war.

On September 17, 1862, Coffin rode down the Hagerstown Pike, and cut across country to the John Hoffman farm. There hundreds were being brought back from the fighting of the corn field and Dunker Church to be treated for their wounds. Coffin graphically described the hospital. He also witnessed the Union advance on the Confederate position in the Sunken Road. He wrote vividly about the colors flying in the advance. Later he told of soldiers singing around the campfire, "Do they miss me at home tonight."

Coffin's approach to reporting from the front is noted in one of his articles, "Antietam Scenes."

When the soldiers are seeking rest, the work of the army correspondent begins. All through the day eyes and ears have been open. The notebook is scrawled with characters intelligible to him if read at once, but wholly meaningless a few hours later. He must grope his way along the lines in the darkness, visit the hospitals, hear the narratives of all, eliminate error, get at probable truth, keeping ever in mind that each general thinks his brigade, each colonel, his regiment, every captain, his company, did most of the fighting.

Coffin was always welcome at army camps and headquarters. He was no critic. He reported the facts, and offered no spin. He had the rare ability of describing a difficult military action in terms that readers could understand. He never hesitated to be at the front, near the scene of combat. Soldiers from his home state of New Hampshire recalled seeing him standing calmly against a tree at Fredericksburg, writing on his note pad while shot and shell were flying.

The writer of this brief account of Coffin's life became acquainted with the correspondent while doing research on Antietam, and then discovered his chapters on Gettysburg.

Coffin joined the Army of the Potomac on the roads to Gettysburg and in Frederick, Maryland on Saturday, June 27, 1863. He observed the build up of the army around the city. He was present at Prospect Hall, Headquarters, Army of the Potomac, when early on Sunday morning, June 28, Major General George G. Meade replaced Major General Joseph Hooker as army commander. Coffin noted the church bells of Frederick were ringing as the command changed.

On Monday, Coffin rode with Major General Winfield Scott and the Union Second Corps on their 30-mile march from the banks of the Monocacy River to Liberty, Johnsville, and Uniontown. On Tuesday, Coffin rode forward to join Major General George Sykes and the Union Fifth Corps on the roads to Gettysburg. This was near Hanover. Coffin rode with Colonel Joshua Chamberlain and Brigadier General Strong Vincent as they made a night march to Gettysburg.

Coffin witnessed the unfolding drama at Gettysburg. He was present for the struggle for Little Round Top. He heard the thunder of the guns during Pickett's Charge across the Emmitsburg Road. When the fighting ended and the guns grew cool, Coffin rode twenty-eight miles in a driving rainstorm with Whitelaw Reid another correspondent. Their destination was Westminster, Maryland. They made the dash in two and a half hours. There at the Union rail depot, the telegraph was tied up with military matters. Coffin then boarded a train for Baltimore, and from that city telegraphed half a column of dramatic news to the *Journal*. Supposedly, this was the first news the nation had of the struggle at Gettysburg. Coffin then took another train to New York, locked himself in a room and wrote for hours the story of the Battle of Gettysburg. The next day, the glorious news covered the Northeast, 122,000 copies of his story were sold.

Returning to Westminster, Coffin obtained his horse from the livery stable and rejoined the army. In a few days he had ridden 100 miles on horseback, and traveled 800 miles by rail. In subsequent articles, Coffin praised Lee's orderly withdrawal and was disappointed by Meade's failure to actively pursue Lee and deliver a crushing blow.

Coffin was with the Army of the Potomac in Washington County, Maryland as Meade faced Lee across the rain swollen Potomac. During this time he spent a day touring the battlefield of Antietam.

The fields and ridges between Sharpsburg and Antietam were still littered with the debris of the battle of the previous September. He saw old boots, shoes, belts, and other military items. He also found many flattened bullets and fragments of shells. Coffin was sickened at the sight of bones, and some skulls protruding from beneath the Maryland soil. Bleached bones of men and horses were seen at many places. Union infantry following Lee also speak of this gruesome scene.

After a short rest, Coffin rejoined the Army of the Potomac for the campaign that marked the beginning of the end. This time there was a new commander in chief of all the Union armies, U. S. Grant. Coffin and Grant were old friends. The general had great respect for the correspondent. As a result, Grant gave Coffin a pass that was good anywhere. The two men often sat on kegs and camp stools and conversed. Grant trusted Coffin completely. What was said in confidence, was kept that way. Coffin was also the first to break the story of the Battle of the Wilderness, that dense patch of forest west of Fredericksburg. Somehow, Coffin once again beat government channels.

Coffin was in South Carolina when the Stars and Stripes were once again raised over Fort Sumter. Then he hastened back to Petersburg for the final drive on Appomattox. He was in Petersburg shortly after it fell on April 2, 1865.

The next day he was in Richmond, part of the city was still burning. While there he met Mr. Lincoln in the streets of the fallen capital of the Confederacy.

When the war concluded, Coffin returned to Boston to rest. Then he began a series of books on the war.

From his prolific pen came *My Days and Nights on the Battlefield* (1864), *Following the Flag* (1865), *Four Years of Fighting* (1865), *Drumbeat of the Nation, Marching to Victory, Redeeming the Republic, Freedom Triumphant, 1888–1891*. The account of Gettysburg appeared in *Marching to Victory*, page 18.

Coffin was a man of many interests. He made a trip to India, China, and Japan. After writing about his trip in *Our New Way Around the World*, Coffin began writing about his boyhood and New England heritage. The books were: *The Boys of '76, The Story of Liberty, Old Times in the Colonies, Building the Nation*, and *Daughters of the Revolution*. Coffin also tried his hand at novels. He wrote on Abraham Lincoln and James A. Garfield.

When not traveling or writing, Coffin was in great demand as a speaker. In those days when evening gatherings were a social and education item, Coffin was one of the leaders. He gave at least 2,000 speeches. In politics, he was elected to the Massachusetts Assembly, and then the Senate. He also found time to serve as the organist in his church in Boston. He was a man of many abilities and perhaps the greatest war correspondent of his day.

The life of this distinguished American came to an end on March 2, 1896. Coffin's death came suddenly, just a few weeks after he and his wife had celebrated their fiftieth wedding anniversary. Eight hundred guests had attended the celebration. None present "could have dreamed that this venerable man would pass away within such a brief period."

Despite a driving rain, Coffin had been at his desk on Saturday, February 28, 1896. On Sunday, he attended two services at the Shawmuth Congregational Church, on the corner of Tremont and Brooklin Streets in Boston. Monday morning he was at his desk when stricken. The *Journal* said, "Apoplexy struck him Monday noon." However, it was an apparent heart attack. His funeral service was held in the Shawmuth Congregational Church.

His passing was mourned in the United States and abroad. The integrity of his writing endeared him to generals and politicians alike, as well as to his readers. His simple signature "Carleton" was all that was needed. During his career he had met Daniel Webster, Mr. Lincoln, U. S. Grant, Phil Sheridan, William T. Sherman and writers like Longfellow, Garrison, William Cullen Bryant and others. On his trips abroad he met Disraeli, William Gladstone and Charles Dickens in England. In France, there was an audience with Louis Napoleon. In Berlin he attended a grand review before the czar of Russia, Bismarck, and the great German general Moltke.

Coffin's name is listed on the War Correspondent's Arch at Gathland, Maryland. However, this writer deserves his biography.

# Chapter I

## *Spring of 1863*

*We approach* the turning point in the great struggle. The months of May and June 1863 will ever stand as the most critical in the history of the mighty conflict. General U. S. Grant had begun his movement to gain the rear of Vicksburg; General Nathaniel Banks was closing around Port Hudson — movements which were designed to open once more the Mississippi to the peaceful commerce of the world, severing Arkansas, Louisiana, and Texas from the other states of the Confederacy.

In Tennessee the Army of the Cumberland, under General Rosecrans, was preparing to move against the Confederates under General Bragg at Tullahoma.

The Army of the Potomac was upon the Falmouth Hills, opposite Fredericksburg. Fifteen thousand soldiers, whose term of enlistment had expired, were returning to their homes. Including the losses at Chancellorsville and those in the hospitals, thirty thousand had disappeared from the ranks. A portion of the loss had been made good by the arrival of new troops, but they were not the veterans who had fought in a score of battles. The many defeats on the Peninsula, at Manassas, Fredericksburg, and Chancellorsville, had had a manifest effect upon the spirits of the army. The soldiers knew that they had fought bravely, but had suffered defeat through the mismanagement at Washington and incompetency of their commanders. They had lost none of their love for the flag, which represented all that was dear to them in life.

The Confederates encamped upon the hills behind Fredericksburg were exultant over the victories they had won, and had good cause for swinging their hats and hurrahing, to feel that they were invincible, and could win a victory against great odds; that General Lee was a great commander, who would lead them ever to victory. They were sad over the death of Stonewall Jackson, and felt that the loss was irreparable. New conscripts were arriving by the thousand to fill up the ranks. Longstreet's corps had returned from Suffolk. The spirits of the troops never had been so high. The people of the South believed that the army under General Lee could not be defeated. The *Richmond Examiner* had this relative to the military strength of the Confederacy: "It never was more ample than now. We have arms for one million soldiers. We have from six hundred to six hundred and fifty thousand effective men. The State militia will give two hundred thousand more. These figures are authentic."[1]

It advocated offensive operations by General

Lee. The time was propitious. The Union army would lose in all sixty or seventy regiments. The Union troops were discouraged. "No treaty of peace is possible save one signed on the enemy's soil," it said.

General Longstreet, the first week in May, was in Richmond, and called upon Mr. Seddon, Secretary of War.

"I have a plan," said Mr. Seddon, "for sending your troops west to Mississippi to join Johnston and attack Grant, who is laying siege to Vicksburg. What do you think of it?"

"I think that there is a better way to relieve Pemberton by bringing the troops under Johnston to Tullahoma, and to hurry forward two of my divisions. With these troops Bragg can crush Rosecrans; then he can march through Tennessee and Kentucky, and threaten the invasion of Ohio. He will have no opposition, and will find provisions everywhere. The result will be the withdrawal of Grant from Vicksburg to head off Bragg."[2]

General Longstreet went on to Fredericksburg and talked the matter over with General Lee.

"To take away your corps will divide my army," said General Lee.

No commander likes to have his troops taken away from him. It is human nature for us to desire to wield all possible power. General Lee was thinking of a plan. He knew that Hooker's army was growing smaller, that regiments were leaving, and that others were not taking their places. It was hardly to be expected that Hooker, after the defeat of Chancellorsville, would make any movement. What should be done? A victorious army after a great victory cannot sit down and do nothing without loss of prestige. If Lee could drive Hooker back to Falmouth, what could he not do with forty thousand additional troops?

"Why not invade Pennsylvania?" General Lee asked.

"Such a movement," said Longstreet, "can be successful if made offensive in strategy but defensive in tactics."

By that he intended to say that if Lee should select his line of march, and the country he intended to occupy, and when it came to a battle to select his ground and wait to be attacked, he would be successful. "The movement," he added, "into Pennsylvania will make a great stir in the North, and Hooker will be compelled to attack you on your chosen ground. You remember Napoleon's advice to Marmont: 'Select your ground and make your enemy attack you.' At Fredericksburg we held Burnside with a few thousand men, crippling and demoralizing his army, while we lost very few. At Chancellorsville we attacked, and Hooker was on the defensive. We dislodged him, but at such a terrible sacrifice that half a dozen such victories would have ruined us."

There were many reasons why General Lee should make a movement somewhere, and especially why he should invade Pennsylvania.

The war from the beginning, except the Battle of Antietam, had been in the seceded states, where the hostile armies had marched to and fro, wasting the country, leaving desolation behind them. The Southern newspapers were calling for a movement of the victorious Army of Northern Virginia into Northern territory, that the people there might feel the burden and woe of war. The state of affairs in the Northern states favored such a movement.

There were so many disloyal men in Ohio and Indiana that General Burnside, who had been sent to Cincinnati to take command there, published an order threatening the arrest of men who should give aid and comfort to the enemy.

On May 5, when Hooker was being driven from Chancellorsville, Burnside sent soldiers to Dayton, who arrested Clement L. Vallandigham. He was tried by a military court. General Burnside paid no attention to the writ of *habeas corpus,* which was issued by a judge of one of the courts, for the civil power had been placed beneath the military. Bayonet instead of civil law ruled. Vallandigham was declared guilty of expressing his sympathies in favor of the enemy. He had been very bitter against the president and the continuance of the war. He was put in prison, but President Lincoln thought it better to send him south to the Confederates.

Mr. Vallandigham had opposed the war from the beginning, and he had rendered great service to the Confederates by his disloyalty to the Union. The newspapers of the South had praised him for what he had done, but he was treated with scant civility in Richmond. He could not render any service to the Confederacy there. These the words of a Richmond newspaper: "He has no claim on our gratitude. He is simply an alien enemy, a prisoner of war, a respectable enemy."[3]

Mr. Vallandigham made his way to Canada, and was soon back in Ohio, the candidate of the Peace Party for governor.

When the war began more men volunteered than were called for, but the wave of patriotism had spent its force; no volunteers came to fill up the ranks, and Congress ordered a draft. It was to go into effect July 1. The Peace Democrats said that the war was a failure.

A great "Peace" Convention was held in New York City, which passed resolutions favoring state rights, for which the South was contending. These the words of one of the resolutions: "Under the Constitution there is no power in the Federal Constitution to coerce the States by military force."

Fernando Wood, of New York City, said, "I am for peace as the only possible hope for the restoration of the Union. I am for peace because the war is a failure. The government has no power to coerce a State. It is a failure because we have undertaken what we cannot perform."

The Democratic Convention of Pennsylvania

denounced the emancipation of the slaves by President Lincoln and the employment of Negroes as soldiers, and passed this resolution:

"The party of fanaticism — or crime, whichever it may be called — that seeks to turn loose the slaves of the Southern states to overrun the North, and to enter into competition with the white laboring masses, thus degrading their manhood by placing them on an equality with Negroes, is insulting to our race, and meets our most emphatic and unqualified condemnation. This is a government of white men, and was established exclusively for the white race."

From the beginning of the war the Confederate government had been looking eagerly across the Atlantic to the countries of Europe for sympathy and help, had received both in arms, ammunition, and supplies of all kinds — had been recognized as belligerents. But that was not enough — they must be recognized as a nation. They had defeated great armies, won brilliant victories. If now they could invade Pennsylvania and defeat the Northern army in its own territory, their friends in England would compel the Queen to recognize the Confederacy as a nation.

If they could defeat the Union army in Pennsylvania, then they could take possession of Baltimore and redeem Maryland; then Washington would be theirs, and they would fling out the Stars and Bars above the dome of the Capitol, and the Confederacy and not the Union would everywhere be hailed as the rising power of the

Western world. The recognition of the Confederacy by France and Great Britain would irritate the North, already angered by the course pursued by the latter country; war would follow, and then the ironclad warships of England's great navy would scatter the fleets blockading Wilmington and Savannah and the Chesapeake like chaff before the wind, and carry desolation to New York and Boston. The troops of Great Britain were already in Canada; Confederate agents were at work in Montreal and Toronto, and opposite Detroit, or Niagara Falls. Once bring about a war between England and the United States, and the independence of the South was certain.

Mr. Roebuck, a member of Parliament, and a great friend of Jefferson Davis, and Mr. Lindsay — also a member of Parliament, who owned a great many ships, and who, we may believe, was not sorry to know that the *Florida* and *Alabama* were burning the ships owned by Americans; that every vessel thus destroyed would bring more grist to his mill and give employment to more British vessels — were both exceedingly active to bring about a recognition of the Confederacy as a nation by England. Mr. Roebuck brought a motion before Parliament to that effect. The debate upon the question was to be held on the evening of the last day of June. The Confederate agent in London had written to Richmond these words: "At least five-sixths of the Lower House and all the peers, with only two

27

or three exceptions, are friendly to us."[4]

Mr. Roebuck was the member from Sheffield, where tall chimneys were pouring out clouds of smoke, engines throbbing, steam hammers pounding, and forges flaming, rolling out thick iron plates for England's navy and for the Confederate navy, and steel for the manufacture of cannon for the Confederates. Mr. Roebuck held a meeting there and induced his constituents to declare in favor of recognizing the South.

Mr. James Spence, of Liverpool, who had a valuable contract with the Confederate government, was organizing "Southern Clubs" and "Associations" to influence the people of England, the working men, the famishing of Lancashire, to declare themselves in favor of recognition. The agent of the Confederacy in London was employing a great number of men to write articles for the newspapers in favor of the South. One morning in May, while the army under General Lee was getting ready to march towards Pennsylvania, the people of London saw on all the billboards along the streets, displayed in bright colors, the British and Confederate flags side by side. The Confederate agent, Mr. Hotze, wrote to Mr. Benjamin in regard to it,

"I have taken measures to placard every available space in the streets of London with representations of our newly adopted flag conjoined with the British flag. I design it to impress the masses with the vitality of our cause, to produce some effect before the motion comes on for discussion."[5]

In the month of March, through the action of Baron Erlanger, of France, Mr. James Spence, of Liverpool, and some of the bankers of London and Paris, a scheme was carried out, the promoters of which expected to make a great deal of money, and at the same time help on the Confederacy. It was known as the Confederate Cotton Loan. Cotton was very cheap in Charleston, Savannah, and Mobile, but it was worth fifty cents a pound or more in Liverpool. The Confederate government was to deliver the cotton at a fixed price, the money thus obtained to go for the payment of the men who were building the ironclad ships of war in the shipyards at Birkenhead, and for cannon, powder, muskets, and supplies.

Persons subscribing to the stock of the company were to have their shares at ninety, the par value being one hundred. The loan was put on the market on March 19, and so adroitly had the agents stimulated the stockbrokers, and those who sympathized with the South, that sixteen million dollars were subscribed for, and the shares commanded a premium of four and one-half percent, and a great many people were disappointed because there were no more shares to be had.[6] Mr. Mason, a Confederate minister, wrote this in his letter to Mr. Benjamin, "It shows, *malgre* all detention and calumny, that *cotton is king at last.*"

Mr. Roebuck and Mr. Lindsay were doing what they could to induce Parliament to vote in favor of Mr. Roebuck's motion, and to bring about the cooperation of Louis Napoleon. Mr. Slidell, in Paris, was working with them. Had we been in the apartments of the emperor in the Tuileries on the afternoon of June 18, we should have been Mr. Slidell and Louis Napoleon consulting together.

"Would it be agreeable for you to see Mr. Roebuck and Mr. Lindsay?" Mr. Slidell asked.

"I would like to see them. You may write to them to that effect."[7]

The emperor waited a moment, and then said, "I think I can do better: make direct proposition to England for joint recognition. . . . I shall bring the question before the Cabinet meeting today."

Mr. Slidell thanked him for his sanction of the contract made for the building of four ships of war at Bordeaux and Nantes, and said,

"I am prepared to build several ironclad ships in France, and I only require your verbal assurance that they shall be allowed to proceed to sea, under the Confederate flag, to enter into contracts for that purpose."

"You may build the ships, but it will be necessary that their destination shall be concealed."

Mr. Roebuck and Mr. Lindsay hastened to Paris and out to Fontainebleau, saw the emperor, and on June 25, while the army of General Lee was in the beautiful Cumberland Valley, in Pennsylvania, making its way towards Gettysburg, Mr. Slidell wrote this to Mr. Benjamin: "The interview of Messrs. Roebuck and Lindsay with the Emperor at Fontainebleau was highly satisfactory. They were authorized to state in the House of Commons that the Emperor was not only willing but anxious to recognize the Confederate States, with the co-operation of England."[8]

This the state of affairs across the Atlantic as the Confederate army — consolidated into three corps, commanded respectively by Longstreet, A. P. Hill, and Ewell; the cavalry by Stuart, and the artillery under Pendleton — prepared to move north, with the confident expectation that they would march in triumph wherever Lee might lead them — possibly through the streets of Philadelphia — and make Washington the capital of the Confederacy.[9] It is quite probable that no such picture presented itself to the imagination of generals Lee or Longstreet, or other Confederate officers; they were able commanders, who made a proper estimate of the difficulties before them, but the enthusiasm of the soldiers was unbounded; they were confident of victory, and that they could reach Philadelphia or New York.

The Army of the Potomac under General Hooker was not so well organized as that of General Lee. It was composed of six corps, giving to a corps commander only half as many men as were controlled by a Confederate corps commander. The horses of the Union cavalry had been badly broken down in the long, hard marches of Stoneman at the time of the Battle of Chancellorsville. General Pleasonton had been placed in command of the cavalry, who set himself to work to obtain new horses.

Deserters from the Confederate army, the last week in May, informed General Hooker that an order from General Lee had been read to the army that the troops were to have long marches and hard fighting in a part of the country where there would be no railroad transportation for them.

On the second day of June a man reached Fortress Monroe from Richmond, who said that General Lee was going to invade Maryland. General Hooker saw that some of the tents which had dotted the landscape on the green hills across the Rappahannock were there no longer. His scouts said that troops were moving from the battlefield of Chancellorsville towards Culpeper; that the Confederate cavalry was encamped in the fields near that town, and that Stuart was getting ready to make a movement; whereupon he determined to find out what General Lee was doing, and ordered pontoon bridges to be laid where Sedgwick crossed the river four weeks before. Again the Sixth Corps, under Sedgwick, marched down to the river, but only a portion of the troops crossed. General Longstreet's troops had just started towards Culpeper, and were at once halted; but General Lee came to the conclusion that General Hooker was not intending to cross the river, and the troops moved on.

General Hooker was troubled by visitors who came to the army. Fathers and mothers wanted to see their sons; wives, their husbands; sisters, their brothers. He sent this to Mr. Stanton, secretary of war:

"My army is more in danger of being taken by the women than by rebels. They arrive by steamboat loads. Yesterday was not a good day for them; only eighteen arrived; of these fifteen held passes from the War Department." In another dispatch, the same day, he gave this information to General Halleck: "As the accumulation of the heavy rebel force of cavalry about Culpeper may mean mischief, I am determined to break it up."

General Hooker wrote to President Lincoln expressing a desire, in case a large portion of the Confederates were to leave Fredericksburg, to cross and fall upon those remaining. This the reply of the president:

"I have but one idea which I think worth suggesting to you, and that is, in case you find Lee coming to the north of the Rappahannock, I would by no means cross to the south of it. If he should leave a rear force at Fredericksburg, tempting you to fall upon it, it would fight in intrenchments and have you at a disadvantage, and so man for man worst you at that point, while his main force would in some way be getting an advantage of you northward. In one word, I would not take any risk of being entangled upon the river, like an ox jumped half over the fence, and, and liable to be torn by dogs front and rear, without a fair chance to gore one way or kick the other."

Again General Hooker sent a dispatch: "Will it not promote the true interests of the cause for me to march to Richmond at once?"

He received this reply: "I think Lee's army, and not Richmond, is your true objective point. If he comes towards the Upper Potomac follow on his flank, and on the inside track, shortening your lines while he lengthens his. Fight him, too, when opportunity offers. If he stays where he is, fret him and fret him."

From the beginning of the war the cry had been throughout the North, "On to Richmond!" McClellan had made the Confederate capital his objective point. General Hooker was doing the same. They had been educated at West Point; but President Lincoln, who never had read a work on military art, by his common sense comprehended and outlined the correct tactics to be pursued in the campaign which Lee, and not Hooker, was inaugurating.

General Stuart, commanding the Confederate cavalry, was proud of his troops. Twice he had ridden round the Union army — once on the Peninsula, and once in Maryland. He held a grand review of them on the smooth fields around Culpeper. The corps was in superb condition, numbering between eleven and twelve thousand. Each soldier regarded it as a grand occasion, with General Lee present to behold their martial bearing. It was a magnificent spectacle. The review over, the brigades moved northward towards the Rappahannock River. The movement for the invasion of the North had begun. In the morning Stuart was to cross the river and move so as to screen the marching of the infantry. Fitzhugh Lee's brigade, under Colonel Mumford, was picketing the river. The order was issued for an early start in the morning.

The railroad leading from Alexandria southwest crosses the Rappahannock River. Brandy Station is the first stopping place south of the river; and Culpeper the second. Two miles below the bridge is Kelley's Ford; two miles above it, Beverly Ford. North of Brandy Station stood St. James's Church, on the road leading to Beverly Ford, on the west side of the road. On the east side is the house of Mr. Thompson, an old-fashioned brick mansion, surrounded by a beautiful grove of trees on a knoll, which overlooked the surrounding fields. The Sixth Virginia Cavalry of Jones's brigade tethered their horses beneath the trees, and the horse artillery parked their guns farther up the road in a field bordered on the north by woods. It is nearly two miles from the ford. Not far from Brandy Station is another large mansion, to which the owner had given the name of Fleetwood, where General Stuart had his headquarters. There is another mansion, that of Mr. Barbour, beautifully situated, with trees around it, upon a swell of land, with broad fields northward and eastward. This the ground on which the Confederate cavalry had bivouacked.

On the afternoon of June 8, while the Confederate cavalry was marching in review, the Union cavalry was moving southwest from its position on the flank of the Union army, accompanied by Ames's and Russell's brigades of infantry. General Pleasonton, with Buford's division of cavalry and Ames's brigade of infantry, was moving in the direction of Beverly Ford; Gregg's cavalry and Russell's infantry were moving towards Kelley's Ford. Duffie's brigade was to cross the river below Gregg, move south to Stevensburg, on the direct road from Fredericksburg to Culpeper, then move to Brandy Station and join the other columns at that point, General Pleasonton supposing the while that Stuart was at Culpeper, five miles beyond Brandy Station.

The Union cavalry halted for a short rest through the brief summer night. No fires were kindled. No Confederate picket or scout saw them. The morning of the ninth dawned. A thick fog, which concealed them, hung along the valley. Davis's brigade of Buford's division was in advance on the road to Beverly Ford. The cavalrymen reached the stream. The Confederate pickets on the southern bank are startled by the sudden splashing of water. Before they can leap into their saddles the Union troops are upon them, capturing nearly all of them.

Had General Buford known that the Confederate batteries were parked near at hand, behind a piece of woods; that the horses were unharnessed and just munching their corn, he might have swooped down upon them, as an eagle upon its prey, and captured four full batteries; but he did not know they were there.

There was a quick harnessing of horses. The skirmishers began firing with their carbines. The Confederates of Jones's brigade were quickly in the saddle. Then came charge and countercharge, firing of pistols, drawing of sabres, a mêlée in which Colonel Davis, of the New York Regiment, was mortally wounded, and the regiment driven; but the Eighth Illinois came up and the Virginians were turned back. The artillerymen drove upon the gallop across the field to St. James's Church, where the guns were wheeled into position. In the flight of the Confederate wagons a desk was jostled from one of them, which the Union soldiers picked up, finding papers which informed Pleasonton of the movement which Stuart was to have made, and of the intention of going beyond the Potomac. There was a saddling of horses in all the Confederate brigades, a sudden breaking up of the camp, and a movement of all the baggage wagons towards Culpeper. General Stuart sent a portion of the troops towards Kelley's Ford, and then rode up to St. James's Church to direct the battle. A messenger came from the direction of Kelley's Ford with the information that a force of Union cavalry was advancing towards Brandy Station from the east; in a few moments they would be in possession of Fleetwood. Colonel Long, of Stuart's staff, sent messengers to Stuart with the news.

The Confederate commander did not credit the information. "Ride back there and see what all that foolishness is about," he said to Major Hart. Then the sound of cannon was heard, and Stuart sent two regiments towards Fleetwood, with their horses upon the run, to find that the Union men of New Jersey, under Colonel Wyndham, were advancing to seize the hill. Stuart began to comprehend the situation. He ordered his troops to fall back from St. James's Church and concentrate at Fleetwood.

A great cavalry battle began for the possession of the hill — a battle very difficult to describe. It was mainly between Gregg's Union division and the whole force of Confederates, with the exception of one brigade. We may think of ten thousand horses, ten thousand fearless riders; the rattling fire of carbines, thundering of cannon; brigades charging upon the guns, flashing of sabres, cutting and slashing, horses and men going down in heaps; yells, curses, thick clouds of smoke and dust, charge and countercharge — a Confederate battery captured and recaptured, again in the hands of the Union troops, again lost, a third time taken, a third time lost — men sabred at the guns, horses and men struggling and writhing; reinforcements of Confederates, the arrival of Rodes's division of infantry, the withdrawal of the Union troops unmolested by the Confederates; six hundred Union and as many more Confederates killed or wounded, three Union cannon the trophies of the Confederates.

They were the guns of the Sixth New York Battery. Of the thirty-six men belonging to the battery twenty-one were either killed, wounded, or were missing. General Gregg reformed his troops on the ground where he had formed them for the attack, and returned across the river. Stuart made no attempt to harass him, for Buford was threatening him from the northwest, where the contest was renewed with great fury. Meanwhile down towards Stevensburg a third conflict was going on between a portion of the Confederates and the Union cavalry under Duffie, which was soon over, was ordered to join General Gregg. With the setting of the sun the Union cavalry recrossed the Rappahannock, having accomplished their object — ascertaining the position of the Confederate forces; that a portion of the infantry was at Culpeper. They had done more than this — they had frustrated the plan of General Lee, the sending of Stuart to menace Washington in his northward movement. Far more than this, for the struggle around Fleetwood was the *making* of the Union cavalry, and the *unmaking* of the Confederate. Up to that hour the Union cavalry had been of little account as a distinct arm of the service; but now organized as a compact body, wielding its strength in solid mass, it became a formidable power, while the Confederate cavalry, from that hour, was on the wane.

"The battle," said a Richmond paper, "narrowly missed being a great disaster to our arms. Our men were completely surprised, and were only saved by their own indomitable gallantry and courage. . . . The Yankees retired slowly, disputing every foot of the ground."[10]

The Union troops were elated by what they had done, while the Confederates were astonished at the persistency, bravery, audacity, and hardihood of the Union cavalrymen. We shall see that in every cavalry engagement, from that hour to the close of the war, the Union cavalry maintained the prestige won in this engagement.

In several histories of the war it is asserted that the attack of the Union cavalry at Brandy Station compelled General Lee to change all his plans; that he had intended to march along the eastern base of the Blue Ridge, while Stuart was to screen the movement by moving towards Washington; but I do not find any evidence that General Lee had marked out such a movement for his main army. General Ewell's troops were then on their way towards the valley of the Shenandoah.

Before the Confederate army started from Culpeper, General Longstreet sent his trusted scout, Harrison, into the Union lines to see what General Hooker was doing.

"Where shall I report to you?" the scout asked.

"Find me wherever I am," was the reply.

General Longstreet gave him some money — not Confederate money, but gold, and the scout disappeared. We shall see him by and by.

The Union troops at Winchester, in the Shenandoah Valley, were in the department commanded by General Schenck, who was at Baltimore. He sent word to General Milroy at Winchester to send his supplies to Harpers Ferry. General Milroy replied that he could hold the place against any force that would probably attack him. He did not know that the whole Confederate army was moving in that direction. He said that there were Union people in Winchester, and that it would be cruel to abandon those who were looking to him for protection. General Schenck replied that he might remain, but must be ready to move at any moment. The War Department at Washington made the mistake of not letting Milroy know that the main body of the Confederate army was at Culpeper — a neglect which resulted in disaster. Milroy telegraphed on the evening of the twelfth for specific orders, but before the orders were ready Ewell's cavalrymen had cut the wires. The next morning Rodes's division of Ewell's corps was at Berryville, east of Winchester, but the Union brigade there escaped to Harpers Ferry. Rodes went on to Martinsburg, north of Winchester, getting between Milroy and the Potomac, while the other divisions of Ewell advanced directly upon the town. Milroy was nearly surrounded. He spiked the guns in the forts on the hills west of the town, abandoned his wagon trains, and at midnight succeeded in escaping with a portion of the troops; but all the sick in the hospital and nearly half of his command were taken prisoners. By staying a day too long the Union army lost more than two thousand men, besides the cannon and wagons. On Sunday evening, while Milroy was getting ready to escape, President Lincoln, in Washington, was sending this dispatch to Hooker: "If the head of Lee's army is at Martinsburg and the tail of it on the plank road, between Fredericksburg and Chancellorsville, the animal must be thin somewhere. Could you not beak him?"

The president sent General Couch to Harrisburg and another officer to Pittsburgh to make arrangements against invasion, and issued a proclamation calling out one hundred thousand militia from Pennsylvania, Ohio, New York, New Jersey, and Maryland. Governor Curtin, of Pennsylvania, also issued a proclamation, informing the people of the state of the threatened invasion. On June 15 I reached Harrisburg. The city was a bedlam. A great crowd of people — excited men, women wringing their hands, and children crying, all with big bundles — were at the railroad station, ready to jump into the cars to escape northward or eastward. Merchants were packing up their goods. There was a great pile of trunks and boxes. Teams loaded with furniture, beds, and clothing rumbled through the streets; wagons were crossing the bridge over the Susquehanna; farmers from the beautiful Cumberland Valley were hurrying their cattle, horses, sheep, and pigs in droves across the river. The banks were sending their money to Philadelphia and New York. The railroads were removing all their cars and engines; housewives secreting their silver spoons and candlesticks. The excitement was very wild when a long train of army wagons came thundering across the long bridge driven by teamsters covered with dust — a portion of the train which Milroy had sent from Winchester — all hurrying as if the Confederates were close upon them. The next morning some of the militia began to arrive — farmers and their sons, clerks from stores, in citizens' dress. It was very laughable to see men wearing long linen coats — "dusters" — and "stove-pipe" hats, armed with old muskets, mounted as cavalrymen, riding pell-mell through the streets. Hundreds of men were at work throwing up entrenchments.

Going from Harrisburg to Baltimore, I found another scene of excitement. General Schenck was in command. A great force of Negroes were at work building breastworks and barricades on the roads west of the city, using hogsheads of tobacco, filling barrels with earth, piling up old wagons, carts, and boxes; cutting down trees, and placing them in front of the breastworks; planting heavy guns on the hills, to command all the avenues of approach.

Twenty-six months before, the Massachusetts troops had fought their way through Baltimore; but now the people were arming for the fight, and the Negroes, as they threw up the yellow earth with their shovels and pounded it down upon the breastworks with mallets, were singing,

"John Brown's body lies a-mouldering
   in the grave;
His soul is marching on."

Only four years had passed since the execution of John Brown; but the nation, the great ideas underlying it, had moved on with a rapidity hardly paralleled in history.

Ed. note: After Chancellorsville and the death of Thomas J. Jackson, Robert E. Lee reorganized the Army of Northern Virginia into three corps commanded by James Longstreet, Richard S. Ewell and Ambrose Powell Hill. Leaving the lines at Fredericksburg, the army moved west, crossed the mountains, and used them as a shield as the troops moved northward toward the Potomac River. The approach march was through the friendly Shenandoah Valley.

# Chapter II

# *Confederate Northward March*

*On the* morning of June 16 Jenkins's brigade of Confederate cavalry advanced from the Potomac into Pennsylvania, through Greencastle, reaching Chambersburg at midnight. Confederate scouting parties went out in all directions collecting what cattle and horses they could find, also all the Negroes, sending them into Virginia to be sold as slaves. The government of which Jefferson Davis was the head was to be established on African slavery — upon the idea that a Negro was to be classed with horses and cattle, having a property value. It mattered not that the Negroes of Pennsylvania were free; they were seized and sent South. It is not probable that General Jenkins, or anyone else, was greatly enriched by the seizure; possibly few, if any, of the Negroes were sold, for slave property in Virginia was rapidly diminishing in value; but the fact remains that the spirit of slavery, the fundamental idea underlying the Confederate government, was displayed by these videttes of the Confederate army. Jenkins, having obtained a large amount of supplies, fell back to join Ewell, who was at Williamsport.

A. P. Hill was marching from Fredericksburg to Culpeper; Longstreet advancing up the eastern slope of the Blue Ridge.

On the upper Potomac General Imboden, with a brigade of Confederate cavalry, was entering Cumberland and destroying the Baltimore and Ohio Railroad to prevent General Kelley, who was in West Virginia with several thousand troops, from coming east.

General Hooker could not determine what Lee intended to do. General Halleck, with all the telegraph wires running into his office in the War Department, could not make out whether Lee was intending to sweep down upon Baltimore or move towards Washington. The Union army was between the Bull Run Mountains and Washington — at Manassas, Centreville, Drainsville — covering Washington, ready to move across the Potomac the moment Lee's movements should indicate his line of advance.

At Harpers Ferry, on Maryland Heights, in a position which Lee could not hope successfully to assail, were ten thousand troops under General French, of little use where they were, but which might be used to excellent advantage by General Hooker. They were not under him, but were under General Schenck's orders, whose headquarters were at Baltimore. General Hooker asked that they might be included in his command, but the request was refused by General Halleck.

In the forts around Washington were thirty thousand troops, under General Heintzelman, to hold the city against attack.

Going down to Yorktown, we see General Keyes with fifteen thousand men in a position to threaten Richmond.

At daybreak, June 17, the Union cavalry, under Pleasonton, was at Manassas Junction. He moved towards Aldie, intending to push northwest to the Blue Ridge to discover what Lee was doing. Kilpatrick, with three of his regiments, led the column up the turnpike. The other regiment of his brigade — the First Rhode Island, two hundred and eighty men, under Colonel Duffie — was directed to go through Thoroughfare Gap in the Bull Run Mountains, to camp at night at Middleburg, five miles west of Aldie.

The Confederate cavalry at the same hour was moving east towards Aldie.

It was two o'clock in the afternoon when Kilpatrick's scouts, advancing towards Aldie, came upon Confederate pickets. The Second New York charged upon them, driving them swiftly through the little village.

The Confederates were of the First, Second, Third, Fourth, and Fifth Virginia. The first three were feeding their horses at Mr. Carter's barn, a mile and a half from Aldie. There was quick saddling, bridling, and forming in column.

A short distance west of Aldie the turnpike divides — one branch running northwest to Snicker's Gap, the other west to Middleburg. Between the roads there is a hill upon which Munford, commanding the Confederates, planted his artillery. His sharpshooters were behind a fence which runs from road to road.

A little stream crosses the road at the foot of the hill, and there is a mill on the road leading to Middleburg. There is a meadow at the foot of the hill and several haystacks. The Union cavalry, to get at Munford, must either charge up the turnpike swept by his cannon, or descend the steep bank, cross the river in the face of his sharpshooters, or make a flank movement.

Kilpatrick saw that he could not charge up the Middleburg Road; that the troops would be annihilated; but the Second New York rushed upon the Confederate's skirmishers and captured several.

Kilpatrick's cannon poured their fire upon the troops along the Snicker's Gap Road, creating confusion in Munford's works. The Fourth New York, Colonel Cesnola, made a charge. For some breach of orders he was under arrest; his sword had been taken from him, but Kilpatrick handed it back in token of his bravery. He was wounded in the mêlée, fell from his horse, and was taken prisoner.

The First Maine, belonging to the first brigade, was sent forward by General Gregg. Kilpatrick rallied his men, and the fight went on.

48

The Union troops attacked with great vigor.

"I never saw men show better spirit," writes Colonel Munford, praising their bravery.

Kilpatrick's persistent attack was gradually folding back Munford's left flank when, to the surprise of the Union troops, the Confederate regiments retired towards Middleburg.

The reason for their sudden abandonment of so strong a position was the arrival of Captain Frank Robertson from Middleburg with an order from General Stuart to fall back to Rector's Crossroads.

The Rhode Islanders under Duffie had passed through Thoroughfare Gap, and were advancing towards Middleburg.

They were within two miles of the town when they came upon the pickets sent out by Stuart to keep watch of the roads. There were carbine shots, a clattering of hoofs, a charge into the town, where Stuart was enjoying the hospitality of his friends, but he leaped into his saddle and escaped.

Duffie had obeyed orders. He was in Middleburg, where he was to stop for the night. He was well aware that he might be attacked in town, and the soldiers barricaded the roads, sending out pickets in all directions.

Stuart halted, sent back his skirmishers to begin the attack, and sent Captain Robertson with the order to Munford, at Aldie, to inform him that a large body of Union cavalry was in his rear, and that he must retreat. Other couriers went upon the gallop with orders to W. H. F. Lee and Robertson to close in upon the enemy.

Colonel Duffie had been ordered, when he reached Middleburg, to send word to Pleasonton. Captain Allen, with two men, started with the dispatch at five o'clock down the main road, but came upon the Fourth Virginia Cavalry retreating from Aldie. Robertson turned through the woods and fields, running against Confederates in every direction. The sun went down, and in the gathering darkness he reached Little River, came upon five Confederates, charged upon them, and compelled them to flee. He followed the river a long distance till he reached the main road, came upon the Union pickets, and was safe. It had been a hazardous, exciting ride. Kilpatrick read the dispatches. He knew the danger closing upon Duffie, but his horses were broken down by the long, hard march and the battle with Munford. He sent the dispatch to Gregg, who carried it to Pleasonton; but Pleasonton issued no orders.

Duffie waited through the long night hours with listening ears to hear the tramping of the expected reinforcements, which never came. He might have retreated, for Robertson had not yet closed the road over which he came. He was a foreigner, born in France, educated in the military schools, under strict discipline to obey orders implicitly. What rebuke would he not receive from Pleasonton were he to retreat! He resolved to hold his ground till reinforcements arrived, not knowing that they would never be sent.

He placed most of his troops in a grove outside of the town. The men were ordered to speak only in whispers. The pickets were out upon the roads. The last gleam of light was fading from the west. Two companies had dismounted, and their horses were tied to trees in a grove, the men lying behind a stone wall bordering the road, across which they had felled a tree. With loaded carbines they waited. As they looked down the road, peering through the darkness, they beheld the advancing Confederate columns, four men abreast. There burst forth a line of light from sixty carbines. Riders and horses went down in a heap. The Rhode Islanders did not stop to load, but out with their revolvers and fired into the struggling mass. The Confederate officers rallied the men, and again they charged, but only to be cut down again by the terrible volley.

The troops attacking Duffie were the Fourth and Fifth North Carolina, new regiments, numbering nearly one thousand, and this was their first battle.

Colonel Duffie makes his way two miles in the darkness, then waits for the morning. His horses have had nothing to eat since they left Manassas Junction. The animals are jaded and hungry, and the men stand by their heads to keep them from whinnying.

Daylight comes, and the men leap into their saddles. The Confederate scouts discover them and fire a volley. Duffie is expecting to hear Kilpatrick's guns or the tramping of his brigade, but discovers instead that W. H. F. Lee's brigade, under Colonel Chambliss, is intercepting his retreat, while Robertson is ready to fall upon his rear. With sabres gleaming he charges upon the Confederates, and gains the road once more. The Rhode Islanders move on two miles towards Hopewell Gap, when they hear the clatter of hoofs behind them. The road is narrow and rugged. They cannot turn and face the oncoming foe. They put spurs to their horses, and the column goes pell-mell along the road, bullets whizzing past them, striking among them; the Rhode Islanders, turning in their saddles, sending shots in the faces of the Virginians. Horses go down, and the riders are trampled by those behind. For six miles the Confederates push on — the ranks of the Rhode Islanders dwindling every moment. Some, when their horses fall, leap over the fences and secrete themselves till the Confederates are gone, then make their way over the mountains eastward.

Color sergeant Robbins, finding that he would be captured, tore the standard from its staff, threw the staff away, thrust the colors into his bosom, was taken prisoner, but escaped. He made his way back to headquarters, took the colors from his bosom and waved them above his head — all the soldiers around swinging their hats at the sight. He received a lieutenant's commission for his heroic service.

When the Confederates gave up the chase all that were left in the column were Colonel Duffie and twenty-seven men. The brave colonel gazed at the little party with the tears rolling down his cheeks.

"My poor boys! My poor boys! All gone! All gone!" were the pathetic words wrung from his heart.

They were not all lost, however, for Lieutenant Colonel Thompson and eighteen men cut their way through the Confederate lines. Lieutenant Brown and several soldiers secreted themselves in the woods till the next day, when Pleasonton's advance enabled them to escape.

Out of the two hundred and eighty, six were killed, twenty wounded, and seventy captured.

On the morning of the nineteenth we see Stuart forming Robertson's and Chambliss's brigades near Middleburg, on a plain, with a grove in the centre of the lines, waiting for the advance of Gregg's two brigades moving along the Aldie Road. The Confederate artillery were on a hill in the rear. A portion of the Union troops dismounted and came down upon their flank, giving so hot a fire that the line was thrown into confusion. The Union centre charged upon those in the grove, driving them, but were driven in turn by the Ninth Virginia, in reserve, and by the artillery fire. Gregg reformed in the woods. Stuart attacked again and again, losing many men, and was compelled at last to give up the effort and retire to another position.

Munford, on the road leading to Snicker's Gap, was compelled to fall back before Buford.

The morning of June 20 dawned. General Stuart had been reinforced by the arrival of Jones's and Hampton's brigades. He sent Jones's north to Munford to hold the road to Snicker's Gap, and formed his other three brigades at Rector's.

General Gregg had been reinforced by the Union infantry of General Vincent's brigade. Gregg was to push Stuart towards Ashby's Gap while Buford folded back his left flank. It was eight o'clock in the morning when the Union troops opened fire upon Stuart, who had formed his line along Cromwell's Creek. Stuart's artillery replied, but was badly cut up by Pleasonton's guns. Vincent advanced so rapidly that Stuart was obliged to abandon two of his cannon.

Stuart rallied his men, but was again compelled to retreat, sending word to Jones and Munford to fall back to Upperville, abandoning the road to Snicker's Gap and concentrating his whole force towards Ashby's.

No one can say just what occurred in the charges and countercharges during the day. Men and horses went down in heaps. There were volleys from carbines, then a rattling fire from revolvers, gleaming of sabres, clouds of dust, mêlées in narrow roads, along stone walls and fences, bloody encounters — a loss of nearly five hundred on each side; but when night came,

Stuart had been pushed back several miles from his ground of the morning.

It was the second great cavalry battle of the war.

Stuart, finding that Pleasonton had a brigade of infantry, sent word to Longstreet, who detailed McLaws's division to assist him; but it did not arrive in season to take part in the fight.

Pleasonton, having accomplished what he was ordered to do, went back to Aldie.

General Stuart had been pushed back from Aldie. It was not a pleasant reflection. Possibly he was feeling the criticisms of the Richmond newspapers over the engagement at Brandy Station. He found that the Union army blocked the route which he had intended to take northward. An idea came to him — possibly suggested by Colonel Mosby — to ride round the Union army, as he had done twice when it was commanded by McClellan. He was an enterprising officer, and loved to do startling things. Such a movement would go far to retrieve the failures of the lost engagements. He submitted the plan to General Lee, who was at Berryville, in the Shenandoah, where, on the evening of June 21, he wrote an order to General Ewell to march to Harrisburg and take possession of the capital if possible. General Ewell was at Williamsport, and his troops on the twenty-second began to cross the river.[1]

The night of the twenty-third was dark and cheerless. General Stuart, near Rector's Crossroads, was asleep beneath a tree, the raindrops pattering upon him, when a messenger reached him from General Lee informing him that Ewell was moving towards Harrisburg, that Early's division was to cross the mountains and march to York. These are Lee's instructions as to Stuart's course:

"If General Hooker remains inactive, you can leave two brigades to watch him and withdraw with the other three; but should he not appear to be moving northward, I think you had better withdraw this side of the mountains tomorrow night, cross at Shepherdstown the next day, and move over to Fredericktown. You will, however, be able to judge whether you can pass around his army without hindrance, doing him all the damage you can, and cross the river east of the mountains. In either case, after crossing the river, you must move on and feel the right of Ewell's troops, give instructions to the two brigades left behind to watch the flank and rear of the army, and (in event of the enemy leaving their front) retire from the mountains west of the Shenandoah, leaving sufficient pickets to guard the passes.[2] I think the sooner you cross into Maryland after tomorrow, the better."

At midnight of June 24, we see three Confederate brigades — Hampton's, Fitzhugh Lee's, and Chambliss's — moving eastward from the town of Salem, through the Bull Run Mountains; but at Haymarket they come upon the Second Corps of the Union army, under Hancock, marching northward. The artillery opens, the Union infantry wheel into line of battle, and Stuart is compelled to turn about, recross the mountain, and when night comes he is back nearly to his starting point. A day has been lost — a very provoking delay to an impatient commander.

General Ewell, with two divisions — Rodes's and Johnson's — were in Chambersburg, with Jenkins's cavalry. General Ewell had lost a leg in the Battle of Groveton, and rode in a carriage when on the march, but in battle was strapped to his saddle. He was well acquainted with the country through which he was marching and around Harrisburg. Before the war, he had surveyed a railroad, and had been stationed at the government barracks in Carlisle, and had been in Chambersburg many times. He demanded of the two authorities a great amount of supplies — five thousand suits of clothing, ten tons of leather, five tons of horseshoes, five thousand bushels of oats, three tons of lead, one thousand currycombs, all the powder and percussion caps in town, one hundred and fifty thousand pounds of bread, five hundred barrels of flour, and twenty-five of sauerkraut, with beans, vinegar, sugar, and other things. They searched houses and stores. One of the officers, Major Todd, of Kentucky, a brother of the wife of Abraham Lincoln,[3] who had joined the Confederates, although his state had not seceded, attempted to go into Doctor Richards's cellar, but was confronted by Miss Richards, the doctor's bravehearted daughter, who seized an axe. "I will split your head open!" she said, and Major Todd thought it prudent not to go any farther. General Ewell had a large package of Confederate treasury notes, and paid liberally for all supplies. General Lee had issued strict orders against plundering. He knew that there was nothing more detrimental to discipline than to permit soldiers to seize whatever they might fancy. The Confederate money was worthless, but there was a form of purchase by the proper authority which preserved the discipline of the army. General Ewell was very strict. Officers who became intoxicated were deprived of their commissions and put into the ranks as privates.

On the morning of June 26 Rodes's and Johnsons's divisions moved northward, while the troops of A. P. Hill arrived at Chambersburg. The whole of the Confederate army, with the exception of Stuart's cavalry, had crossed the Potomac. General Hill was well acquainted with the country, for he too had been at Carlisle before the war. He knew many of the citizens, and asked about them. While he was resting in the public square the citizens saw a man wearing a suit of gray, with stars on the collar, sitting at rest in his saddle — a gentleman with a benevolent and kindly face with a shade of sadness and anxiety, accompanied by a large number of officers — ride up the street. It was General Lee, who talked with General Hill[4] a few minutes and then rode eastward to Mr. Messersmith's farm, where his headquarters were established in a beautiful grove.

While General Lee was going into camp Early's division was passing through Gettysburg. General Early demanded from the inhabitants sixty barrels of flour, seven thousand pounds of bacon, and twelve hundred pounds of sugar; he wanted also forty bushels of onions, five hundred hats, and one thousand pairs of shoes. If he could not have these he must have ten thousand dollars in money. As he was ordered to proceed at once to York, he could not stop to collect the articles; besides, York was a much larger town, situated in a rich and fertile section of the country, where he could make larger reprisals, with the probability that the people would comply with his demand, rather than that he should burn the place.

While they were marching through the town, and while General Lee was resting beneath the grateful shade of the oaks near Chambersburg, Mr. Huber, of Chambersburg, was making his way along secluded roads, eluding the Confederates, obtaining horses, riding fast, reaching the road, and at daylight on the morning of the twenty-seventh he is in the capital at Harrisburg, narrating to Governor Curtin what he has seen, and the telegraph is conveying the information to Washington, and out to General Hooker.[5]

The Army of the Potomac, meanwhile, had been moving. General Hooker was swinging it on a much smaller circle than that of the Confederates. He was covering Washington until he could see just what General Lee was intending to do. He was moving his troops northward, east of the South Mountain range, holding all the passes. On Wednesday, the twenty-fifth, he placed the First, Third, and Eleventh Corps under the command of General Reynolds, constituting the left wing of the army. They crossed the Potomac at Edwards Ferry. While they were crossing, the Second Corps was turning Stuart back at Haymarket. All the troops were in position to cross the river.

Saturday, June 27, General Hooker was at Frederick. The three corps under Reynolds were at Middletown. All the troops were north of the Potomac. General Lee was resting beneath his tent in the grove at Chambersburg. All of Longstreet's and Hill's troops were near him. Early was on the march towards York, Rodes's division at Carlisle, Johnson's between Chambersburg and Carlisle.[6] General Stuart had started once more, riding southeast around the southern end of Bull Run Mountains, crossing the railroad from Alexandria to Culpeper at Bristoe Station, going on in the same direction, crossing the Occoquon River — marching till he was almost within sight of the Potomac River — then turning north, crossing the Occoquon again west of Mount Vernon, passing through Fairfax Court House, where Hampton's brigade came upon a squadron of Union cavalry, about one hundred men, under Major Remington. Most of the Union cavalrymen were captured. It had been a long, circuitous march to gain the rear of Hooker's army. Had Stuart waited at Rector's Crossroads, he could have been at the same place on the evening of the twenty-seventh and saved a day's march, for the Union army had moved on. Stuart reached the Potomac fifteen miles above Washington; but the river had risen, and the water was so deep that the artillerymen were obliged to take the ammunition out of the chests and hold the cartridges in their arms while crossing. All through the night the brigades were splashing through the water, the rear guard gaining the Maryland shore just at daylight on Sunday morning.

I was in Frederick, arriving there before any of the troops, with the exception of the cavalry — ten thousand, under Pleasonton. There was no halting of the cavalry, but the great column moved on through the streets and out upon the roads leading northward towards Pennsylvania. Then came the Reserve Artillery, jarring the ground with the rumbling of the carriages. General Hooker had so directed the movement of the infantry that they did not enter the town, but were moving either east or west of it — all towards the north.

While the cannon were rolling over the pavements there came the pealing of church bells calling the people to worship. The birds were singing in the orchards, the air fragrant with flowers; upon all the surrounding hills the wheat was ripening. It was a memorable Sunday morning, for a special train had arrived in the night from Washington bringing Colonel Hardie with a letter to General Hooker and another to General George G. Meade, who was commanding the Fifth Corps. General Hooker had again asked that General French, who was at Harpers Ferry with eleven thousand men, be placed under his command, to be joined to the Twelfth Corps, commanded by General Slocum, that the force of more than twenty thousand men might be sent to gain the rear of General Lee and cut his communications with Virginia. General Halleck would not consent that the troops under General French should be withdrawn from Harpers Ferry; he considered it a place of great importance. General Hooker thereupon had asked to be relieved of any further command of the army, and President Lincoln had acceded to his request, and had appointed General Meade, who was a native of Pennsylvania, and who had rendered excellent service as a division and corps commander.

I saw General Meade a few moments after the appointment had been placed in his hands. It was a surprise. No one had thought that there could be such an event. It was a position of great responsibility which had come to him. He knew nothing as to what General Hooker's plan were; he only knew that the army was marching; that before many days there must be a great battle.

The army, aside from the troops of his own corps, knew very little about him. He was standing with bowed head and downcast eyes, his slouched hat drawn down, shading his features. He seemed lost in thought. His uniform was the worse for wear from hard service; there was dust upon his boots. As a faithful soldier, loyal to duty, he accepted the great responsibility; while General Hooker, shaking hands with him and with his officers, with the tears coursing down his cheeks, bade them farewell, entered the cars, and went to Baltimore, as he had been directed. Patriotic, tender, and pathetic were the words of Hooker to the army in his brief farewell:

"Impressed with the belief that my usefulness as commander of the Army of the Potomac is impaired, I part from it, yet not without the deepest emotions. The sorrow of parting with the comrades of so many battles is relieved by the conviction that the courage and devotion of this army will never cease nor fail; that it will yield to my successor, as it has to me, a willing and hearty support. With the earnest prayer that the triumph of this army may bring successes worthy of it and the nation, I bid it farewell."

Dignified, modest, and unassuming the words of General Meade in his short address:

"The country looks to this army to relieve it from devastation and the disgrace of hostile invasion. Whatever fatigues and sacrifices we may be called upon to undergo, let us have in view constantly the magnitude of the interests involved, and let each man determine to do his duty, leaving to an all-controlling Providence the decision of this contest."

General Meade made a tender and graceful tribute to General Hooker, "whose name must ever be conspicuous in the history of the achievements of the army."

Notwithstanding the defeat at Chancellorsville, the soldiers liked General Hooker, and he had regained in a good degree their confidence; but their loyalty was not to men, it was to the flag, to what it represented — the government of the people, the highest advancement which man had attained; and so, without complaint at the action of President Lincoln in appointing General Meade, they moved on in obedience to orders, knowing that every step brought them nearer to the Confederate army.

General Halleck did not like General Hooker, and had refused his request regarding the troops at Harpers Ferry, but, upon the appointment of General Meade, those troops were placed under his command. General Hooker remained at Baltimore three days, but hearing nothing from General Halleck, went to Washington, where he was summarily arrested by General Halleck, because he had not obtained permission to do so. The course pursued by General Halleck, in granting to Meade what he had refused to Hooker, and in ordering Hooker's arrest, aroused much indignation throughout the country.

During the evening of Sunday a wagon train, loaded with supplies, was moving west from Rockville, Maryland, when the teamsters saw a body of Confederate cavalry swooping down upon them. It was Stuart, who captured one hundred and twenty-five wagons. A little later, the telegraph between Washington and Frederick ceased to work. Stuart was cutting the wires. The Confederate cavalrymen were within a few miles of Washington and Baltimore; but Stuart, instead of menacing those cities, was moving north with the captured train, reaching the Baltimore and Ohio Railroad on Monday morning, tearing up the track and burning a bridge, and then hastening on.

Sunday was not a day of rest to Early's Confederate division, which was entering York, Pennsylvania, at eleven o'clock in the forenoon, demanding five hundred barrels of flour, several tons of bread, thirty thousand bushels of corn, one thousand hats, one thousand pairs of shoes, a great variety of articles, and one hundred thousand dollars in money, to be delivered at four o'clock, or the town would be set on fire. No resistance had been offered. One of the citizens had gone out several miles to inform Early that he could take peaceable possession of the place. The citizens could obtain only twenty-eight thousand dollars. Early thereupon issued an address, exalting his humanity in not setting the town on fire. He trusted that the humane treatment they had received at his hands would induce them "to shake off the revolting tyranny which they were undergoing."

General Gordon's brigade of Georgians pushed on to Wrightsville, thirteen miles on the western bank of the Susquehanna. The Georgians swung their hats when they beheld the gleaming water of the great river. They were to seize the wooden bridge, a mile long, which spanned the stream between Wrightsville and Columbia. General Early was thinking of crossing the river, passing through Columbia, and sweeping up the eastern bank thirteen miles farther, while Jenkins's cavalry and Rodes's division advanced from Carlisle, thus seizing Harrisburg. But Colonel Frick, of the Pennsylvania troops, was at Wrightsville. He had picked up a few Union soldiers who had been in battle, and who were not to be frightened by the whirring of shot and shell. He had some militia, and among them a company of colored troops. The citizens of Columbia were hard at work throwing up entrenchments west of Wrightsville; they had no cannon. Colonel Frick was to hold the place as long as he could, then retreat, blowing up a span of the bridge. Early planted his cannon at half-past four. For more than an hour the men under Colonel Frick held their ground, when, seeing that the Confederates, who outnumbered them nearly ten to one, were about to gain his flanks, Colonel Frick ordered his men to retreat across the bridge. The fuses were lighted; the powder exploded, but did not blow up the span, and then the bridge was set on fire. It was a magnificent spectacle — the great wooden structure burning through the evening, illuminating all the surrounding country.

Monday morning, the twenty-ninth, dawned. General Lee was still encamped in the grove near Chambersburg. He was wondering what had become of General Stuart. He did not know where he was, neither did he know the whereabouts of the Union army. A physician of Chambersburg who went to see him about a horse that had been taken from him, says:

"Never have I seen so much emotion depicted upon a human countenance. With his hand at times clutching his hair, and with contracted brow, he would walk with rapid strides for a few rods, and then, as if he bethought himself of his actions, he would, with a sudden jerk, produce an entire change in his features and demeanor, and cast an inquiring gaze on me, only to be followed in a moment by the same contortions of face and agitation of person."[7]

General Lee, with an instinct common to officers and soldiers alike in both armies, knew that a great and decisive hour was approaching. He was in a strange country, experiencing such difficulties as all the Union commanders had encountered in Virginia and Tennessee and Mississippi. He had made preparations for a movement to Harrisburg; he was ignorant of the whereabouts of the Union army, and supposed it was still in Virginia.[8] He had relied upon Stuart to keep him informed as to the movements of the Union troops, but had received no information. Many Southern writers have censured Stuart for the line of march taken by him, claiming that by going round in rear of the Union army he placed himself in a position where it was impossible for him to communicate with General Lee; but we are not to lose sight of the fact that Stuart left two brigades, Robertson's and Jones's, to watch the passes of the Blue Ridge, and that they were in position to send word to Lee; besides, Imboden's large brigade and Jenkins's brigade were near at hand, and portions of them might have been sent east of the mountains to watch for any advance of the Union army.

In Virginia General Lee had always received quick information of the movements of the Union army from the people as well as from his cavalry; but now he was in a country where the people were sending information of his movements, but who had no information to give in regard to the movements of the Union army.

It was ten o'clock on Monday evening when the pickets of Longstreet's corps saw a man approaching their lines, whose movements were so suspicious that they arrested him.[9] His clothes were covered with mud — he was very dirty, as if he had been on a long tramp. It was the scout Harrison, whom Longstreet had sent into the Union lines from Culpeper (p. 40). He had been with the Union army all the way up to Frederick. When he saw the troops entering that town he had started to find his commander, and was tired out by his long tramping. General Longstreet was asleep, but was awakened to hear his story, and sent the scout to General Lee. It was not far from midnight when the scout rehearsed his tale to the Confederate commander in chief in his tent beneath the oaks, just out from Chambersburg.

We come to an interesting hour. It was startling information. General Lee did not know that the Union army had crossed the Potomac. He had issued orders to move to Harrisburg. Ewell, with two divisions, was advancing down the valley, and was at Carlisle, thirty miles away. Early was at York, on the banks of the Susquehanna, sixty miles distant. He did not know where Stuart was — had heard nothing from him since leaving Virginia, but at that hour Stuart was nearly sixty miles away, while Robertson's and Jones's cavalry brigades were still in Virginia. "The information changed," says Longstreet, "the whole plan of the campaign."

Before daylight, couriers were riding north of Carlisle with orders for Ewell to turn back, and southward into Virginia for Robertson and Jones to hurry to Chambersburg.[10] Orders were issued to Hill to move over the mountain along the turnpike towards Gettysburg, and for Longstreet to follow. It was a movement for the concentration of the army.

When General Meade assumed command of the Union army on Sunday, he only knew that

General Lee was in the vicinity of Chambersburg. On Monday he learned that Early was at Wrightsville, that Ewell was threatening Harrisburg, and that a large force of Confederates was at Chambersburg. He could only surmise what Lee intended to do, and must so move that he could concentrate his army at any point; to that end the different corps moved north, spreading out like a fan; the Sixth Corps took the road to Westminster, with Gregg's division of cavalry, to swing out upon the right flank, while Buford's division hovered on the left, the troopers riding up the byways amid the mountains to ascertain the movements of the Confederates.

Like two storm clouds the two armies, on the last day of June, were approaching each other. I was riding with General Hancock, commanding the Second Corps. We came to a farmhouse, where, by the gateway, with roses in bloom around them and pinks perfuming the air, stood a mother and her daughters, with loaves of bread in baskets and jars of apple butter — the mother cutting great slices of bread, the daughters spreading them with the sauce and presenting them to the soldiers.

"Hurrah for the mother! Three cheers for the girls!" shouted the soldiers, as they took the luscious gifts and hastened on.

I joined the Fifth Corps. While passing through the town of Liberty a farmer rode into the village. The load in his wagon was covered with a white cloth.

"What have ye got to sell, old fellow? Ginger-bread, eh?" said a soldier, raising the cloth and peeping in. "What do ye ask?"

"I haven't any to sell."

"Haven't any to sell! What are ye here for?"

The farmer made no reply.

"See here, old fellow, won't ye sell me a hunk of gingerbread?" said the soldier, producing an old wallet.

"No."

"Well, you are a mean old cuss. It would be serving you right to tip up your old cart. Here we are marching all night and all day to protect your property and fight for ye. We haven't had any breakfast, and may not get any dinner. You are a set of mean cusses round here, I reckon."

The farmer stood up on his wagon seat, took off the tablecloths, and said:

"I didn't bring my bread here to sell. My wife and daughters sat up all night to bake it for you, and you are welcome to all I've got, and I wish I had ten times as much. Help yourselves."

"See here, my friend, I take back all the hard words I said about you," said the soldier, shaking hands with the farmer, who sat on his wagon with tears rolling down his cheeks.

At daybreak on this last day of June we see Buford's division of Union cavalry, Gamble's and Devin's brigades, leaving their bivouac at the little village of Fountain Dale amid the mountains, and moving north. Through the night the Union pickets have seen lights gleaming in the distance around the town of Fairfield — the fires of Davis's brigade of Heth's division of Hill's Confederate infantry; and General Buford discovers that the Confederates are passing through the mountain defiles, and moving northeast in the direction of Gettysburg. He had but one battery, and instead of attacking, moves southeast to Emmitsburg, near which he finds the First Corps, under General Reynolds, who commands his own, the Third, and Eleventh Corps, forming now the left wing of the army.

"Move to Gettysburg and hold it," is the order of Reynolds, and we see the cavalry going north over a turnpike, passing through Gettysburg, turning west and unsaddling their horses in the fields and beautiful groves around the Theological Seminary, driving before them a small body of Pettigrew's Confederate infantry which was moving east into Gettysburg to obtain supplies, but which fell back to Cashtown, sending word to Hill that the Union cavalry was at Gettysburg.

At this evening hour on the last day of June, General Meade is at Taneytown, thirteen miles southeast of Gettysburg. The First Corps of his army, under General Reynolds, is resting at Marsh Run, seven miles south of Gettysburg, the soldiers boiling their coffee beneath the shade of the trees, the artillerymen watering their horses in the stream. The Eleventh Corps, under General Howard, is in the fields around Emmitsburg, three miles farther south, on the boundary between Maryland and Pennsylvania.

The Third Corps, under General Sickles, is at Bridgeport, five miles southeast of Emmitsburg, on the road to Taneytown.

The Second Corps (General Hancock) is with General Meade at Taneytown; the Twelfth Corps (General Slocum) is at Littlestown, six miles northeast of Taneytown; the Fifth Corps (General Sykes) at Union Mills, seven miles east of Taneytown; the Sixth Corps (General Sedgwick) at Manchester, seven miles still farther east, thirty-two miles from Gettysburg.

On the morning of June 30 Ewell's three Confederate divisions started towards Gettysburg, Rodes's and Johnson's marching south from Carlisle; Early southwest over the turnpike from York; marching so rapidly that in the evening they were at Heidlersburg, only ten miles from Gettysburg. Hill had crossed the mountains with Heth's and Pender's divisions. Andersons's division was on the western slope at Greenwood. Longstreet moved to Greenwood with Hood's and McLaws's divisions — ten miles east of Chambersburg — leaving Pickett's division to guard the long trains of supplies and ammunition. General Lee had left the grove at Chambersburg, and was at Greenwood with Longstreet, his trusted lieutenant. The Confederate army, aside from the cavalry, was much better concentrated than the army of General Meade.

It probably never will be known just how many men there were in the Confederate and Union armies advancing towards Gettysburg. The official returns do not give the true numbers, on account of changes made after taking the returns and before the arrival at Gettysburg.

When the Confederate army reached Chambersburg, Mr. Messersmith, cashier of the bank, undertook to ascertain the number, making a tally of each hundred. An officer saw what he was doing and ordered him to stop. Mr. Messersmith bowed, but went to his barn, obtained a hundred kernels of corn, holding them in his hand in his trousers pocket, dropping a kernel for every hundred. When his hand was empty, ten thousand had passed. Then he gathered them up and dropped them again. Through the day he stood upon the steps of the bank counting the passing troops. He estimated the number at sixty thousand, which did not include Early's division or Stuart's cavalry. The Confederate army had advanced slowly from the Potomac, and the ranks had been kept closed. There were few stragglers.

The Union army had made rapid marches after crossing the Potomac, and a great many soldiers had straggled from the ranks. I saw many drop by the roadside on the march from Frederick northward. The week after the battle I rode from Westminster, northwest of Baltimore, to Boonsboro, beyond South Mountain, and I saw many Union soldiers who had straggled, and who had not returned to their regiments. From the many stragglers there seen, I judge that not less than five thousand, and possibly many more than that number, had dropped from the ranks. The Confederate cavalry, including Imboden's and Jenkins's brigades, numbered not far from thirteen thousand; the Union cavalry, about eleven thousand.[11] The Confederate army had two hundred and eighty-seven cannon, the Union army three hundred and seventy. It is probable that the Confederate army numbered not far from seventy-five thousand, the Union army about eighty thousand.[11]

While the cavalry of General Buford were unsaddling their horses in the grove around the Lutheran Theological Seminary on the last night of June, there was another scene far away across the Atlantic in the great hall of the House of Commons, where Mr. Roebuck was delivering a speech favoring the recognition of the Confederate States as a nation by England.[12] These his words: "We should acknowledge the South because they have won their freedom, and because it is for our interest. It is not Richmond that is now in peril, but Washington; and if there be terrors anywhere it is in the minds of the merchants of New York [cheers]."

Far into the night the discussion went on. Nearly all the speakers believed that the Southern states would gain their independence; the people of the South had their sympathies, but the time had not come for decisive action; it would be better for England to wait a little and see what would come from the invasion of Pennsylvania.

Off the coast of Brazil, in South America, in the great highway of commerce, where the ships of all nations were furrowing the Atlantic, the CSS *Alabama* was waiting for her prey, lighting the ocean with burning vessels, sweeping the commerce of the United States from the seas, securing the carrying trade of the world to the merchants, shipbuilders, and sailors of Great Britain.

The armies of France are in the city of Mexico, and Louis Napoleon is preparing a throne for Maximilian of Austria. If the impending battle shall result in defeat to the Union army, what attitude will Great Britain and France assume towards the United States? Will they not recognize the Confederacy as a nation? We approach a great turning point in the history of our country.

# Chapter III

## *An Unexpected Battle*

*It is* a beautiful grove of oak and hickory crowning the ridge upon which stands the Lutheran Theological Seminary, three-fourths of a mile west of the village of Gettysburg. Going northwest along the Chambersburg Turnpike from the ridge, we come to Mr. McPherson's farmhouse and large barn. Passing this we descend to Willoughby Run and the tollgate; crossing the run, ascending a gentle slope a quarter of a mile, and we are at the tavern of Mr. Herr.

By the side of the turnpike, a few roads north, is an unfinished railroad, with a cut through Seminary Ridge nearly twenty feet deep, and there is an embankment partly completed across Willoughby Run.

We look over a beautiful country — broad and fertile fields which, on the midsummer days of 1863, were waving with wheat ripe for the reaper, or clover waiting for the mower.

Through the night couriers were coming and going over all the roads around Gettysburg. The pickets of Buford's cavalry were along Willoughby Run. General Buford, from the cupola of the seminary, looking westward, could see the glimmering campfires of A. P. Hill's corps in the fields of Cashtown. General Buford had but two brigades — Gamble's and Devin's — less than three thousand men, with only one battery of artillery, A, Second United States, Captain Tidball, commanded by Lieutenant Calef. He had been ordered to hold Gettysburg, and he placed Gamble's brigade south of the turnpike and Devin's north of it, secreting the horses in the woods, and deploying the men as infantry, resolving to make Willoughby Run his line of defense. He was very sure that the Confederates would advance from Cashtown and attack him in the morning. He sent his videttes out to Marsh Creek, nearly two miles, and had pickets on all the roads, and sent messengers to General Reynolds, of the First Corps, who was seven miles south, also on Marsh Run — the same stream — and a messenger to Taneytown, informing General Meade that he was confronted by the Confederates.[1]

Before the sun appeared above the eastern horizon the troops of Heth's division of A. P. Hill's corps of Confederates were awakened by the morning drumbeat.[2] They ate their breakfast and filed into the turnpike, and began their march eastward towards Gettysburg. At Marsh Run they came upon Buford's videttes, who fell back to Willoughby Run.

It was eight o'clock, and the sun's rays were glinting from the spires of the town, when a cavalryman came riding down the hill past Herr's Tavern, informing Buford that the Confederates were coming.[3] A few moments later and Marye's battery from Fredericksburg, Virginia, belonging to Pegram's battalion of artillery, came to a halt in front of the tavern. The Confederates could see men in blue uniforms in the fields east of Willoughby Run. The cannoneers jumped from their limbers, wheeled their cannon, and sent a shell whirring across the stream.

A moment later Lieutenant Rodes, commanding two guns of Calef's battery in the road on the crest of the ridge north of McPherson's house, gave an order to fire, and a shell went flying westward towards Herr's Tavern. The great battle had begun. No one had selected the ground. Buford had been directed to hold Gettysburg, and was obeying. Heth had been ordered to advance to Gettysburg, and was also obeying orders. General Lee, when in Fredericksburg, before setting out to invade Pennsylvania, had determined to fight a defensive battle, but the conflict had begun of itself upon ground which no one had selected; so in war events shape themselves, overturning well-laid plans.

Calef placed the centre section, two guns, under Sergeant Newman, in the field south of the turnpike, and sent Lieutenant Pugel, with the other two cannon, through McPherson's woods, farther south, and the cannonade opened vigorously.[4]

General Heth directed General Archer, with

his brigade, to file into the field south of the tavern, and General Davis to deploy between the turnpike and the railroad on the north. The Confederates descended the slope towards Willoughby Run, when suddenly from the grove, from fence and thicket, there came a volley of musketry which arrested their advance. The fire was so determined that General Heth believed he was confronted by a column of infantry.

General Heth sent word to General Hill that he had encountered a strong force, and Hill ordered General Pender to advance. While that division was on its way from Cashtown the cannonade went on between Calef's six guns and seventeen Confederate cannon, accompanied by a rattling fire of musketry along Willoughby Run.[5] From the cupola of the seminary General Buford looks down upon the scene, casting anxious glances over the green fields southward. He sees a group of horsemen coming up the Emmitsburg Road, and still farther away the sunlight glints from gun barrel and bayonet. The foremost horseman is General Reynolds, followed by his staff, and the dark column is Wadsworth's division. Buford has already sent a cavalryman to guide them. They leave the turnpike at Mr. Codori's house and turn northwest across the fields. General Reynolds hastens to the seminary and shakes hands with Buford. Last evening he was sad and dejected, as if weighed down with a sense of great responsibility, or of a premonition that his life work was almost ended; but now every sense is quickened. He ascends the stairs to the cupola and sweeps the landscape with his glass. Northward is a beautiful plain dotted with farmhouses, crossed by fences, traversed by the roads north to Carlisle, northeast to Harrisburg, northwest, over Oak Ridge, to Mummasburg; behind him is the town; east of it, Cemetery Hill, the marble headstones standing out clean and white in the morning sun; beyond it, crowned with a forest, is Culp's Hill; southward from the cemetery is Zeigler's grove of oaks and a gentle ridge, changing to a rocky, wooded hill — Little Round Top — with Great Round Top beyond. It is an enchanting landscape. Southward from the seminary extends the ridge upon which it stands, thickly covered with oaks. Westward, almost beneath him, are Buford's hard-pressed lines, with Calef's battery sending shot and shell across Willoughby Run, while on the Chambersburg pike are the advancing columns of Pender's division.

At last, after many days of weary marching, the two armies are to meet by chance upon a field which Buford, by the terms of his orders from Reynolds, has seen fit to hold. Couriers ride down the Emmitsburg Road with orders from Reynolds to the other two divisions of the First Corps, and to General Howard, commanding the Eleventh, to hasten to Gettysburg.

Marsh Run, upon which Buford's pickets began the fight, runs southeast, and crosses the

Emmitsburg Road five miles south. Wadsworth's division had bivouacked on its banks — Meredith's brigade on the north, Cutler's on the south side of the stream. General Cutler, ever prompt, was ready when the hour for marching arrived. He crossed the bridge and took the lead of the column, the soldiers carrying one day's rations in their haversacks and sixty rounds in their cartridge boxes.

A cavalryman comes clattering down the turnpike with an order to General Wadsworth to march across the fields upon the double-quick.

"Pioneers to the front!" is the order, and the men who carry axes run ahead, tear down the rails, and the column turns into the field.[6]

"Load at will! Forward! Double-quick!" and the men go upon the run through the meadows, the pioneers clearing the way, Hall's Second Maine Battery dashing ahead, the horses upon the gallop, ascending the hill, passing the seminary, wheeling into position on the north side of the turnpike in line with Calef's.[7]

As the brigade goes across the fields they see an old gray-haired man who fought in the Mexican War coming across the meadow from his small one-story house on the Chambersburg Road at the western end of the town. He has his gun in hand, and joins the ranks of the One Hundred and Fiftieth Pennsylvania Regiment. It is John Burns, who does not wait to be enrolled, but fights valiantly till wounded.

In the ranks of Baxter's brigade, advancing

from Emmitsburg, is a boy from that town marching with the men of the Twelfth Massachusetts — J. W. Weakly. He has obtained a gun, a soldier's cap, and a blue blouse. His blood is up, and he is determined to fight the Confederates. He is thin and pale, and not very strong. He wants to be mustered in as a soldier, and Colonel Bates, commanding the regiment, has accepted him. Before night he will be lying upon the field, his young blood staining the green grass from a wound in his right arm and another in his thigh.

When Baxter's brigade reached Codori's house and turned into the fields they gave a cheer. Some of the men who had been detailed to guard the wagon expressed their dissatisfaction.[8]

"What is this row about?" asked General Baxter.

"We want to go to our regiment if there is to be any fighting."

"Oh, is that it? Very well; if that is the case, you are just the men I want." Across the fields they go upon the run to join their respective commands.

While Cutler's and Meredith's men are coming up the eastern slope of the ridge, let us go over to Willoughby Run and take a look at Heth's advance. South of the turnpike Archer's brigade, finding only dismounted cavalrymen in front of them, has passed on, crossed the stream, and is driving Gamble step by step back towards the seminary. North of the turnpike Davis's brigade is sweeping across the fields, compelling Devin to fall back. From Herr's Tavern, Pegram's sixteen guns are sending shot and shell upon Calef's and Devin's unprotected men. Pender's division is deploying in the fields by Herr's Tavern.

At this moment Archer's men were advancing upon one of the guns of Calef's battery, shooting four of Sergeant Newman's horses, but the gunners took hold of the cannon and dragged it back.

General Reynolds leads Cutler's brigade in person into position, stationing the Seventy-sixth New York Regiment, Fifty-sixth Pennsylvania, and One Hundred and Forty-seventh New York north of the railroad excavation, while General Wadsworth places the Fourteenth and Ninety-fifth New York south of it, to support the battery.

Up through the green field advances Davis's Confederate brigade, following the retreating cavalry. Before Cutler's regiments are in position men begin to fall from the ranks. The atmosphere is thick with the drafting cannon smoke. General Cutler with his glass looks down towards Willoughby Run.[9]

"Is that the enemy?" Colonel Hoffman, of the Fifty-sixth Pennsylvania, inquires.

"Yes."

"Ready! Right oblique! Aim! Fire!" are his orders, and a volley crashes upon the air; a volley from Davis's Confederate brigade is the response.

General Meredith's brigade followed Cutler's in the march from Marsh Run.[10] Cutler's had passed up the ridge and taken position north of the seminary. A staff officer sent by Reynolds conducted Meredith into position. The Second Wisconsin was in advance upon the run, and passed south of the house of Mr. Shultz, into the woods of McPherson, coming forward by company into line, the men loading their guns while upon the run.[11] The cavalry were falling back. The Confederates under Archer had crossed Willoughby Run, picking their way through the thicket and tangled vines along its banks, and forming on the eastern side. In an instant the conflict began at close range, the Second Wisconsin firing a volley before the other Union regiments came into position. The volley was almost simultaneous with that of the Fifty-sixth Pennsylvania.

It was ten o'clock — probably a few minutes past the hour. General Reynolds, having placed Cutler's brigade in position up by the turnpike with Hall's battery, relieving Calef's, came riding down through McPherson's field into the woods. General Doubleday, who had commanded the third division of the First Corps, but who had been appointed by Reynolds to command the corps while he directed the movements of the left wing, came galloping with his staff over the fields from Codori's house to the

Fairfield Road, stopping there, and sending a staff officer to Reynolds for instructions. "Tell Doubleday that I will hold the Chambersburg Pike, and he must hold the road where he is."[12] The air is thick with bullets. Reynolds is a conspicuous figure on his horse. The Confederates are but a few rods distant, and can see that he is giving directions. A soldier singles him out, and fires a bullet which passes through his brain. He falls from his horse dead, speaking no word, uttering no cry. At the beginning of the battle the Union troops lost a commander of such eminence and ability that President Lincoln had thought of appointing him to the command instead of Meade.[13]

The sad news runs along the lines of the "Iron Brigade," as Meredith's has been called, and the men are determined to avenge his death.[14] Archer's Confederate brigade is before them; it had crossed Willoughby Run. "Forward! Charge!" was Meredith's command, and the line went forward, striking Archer's line partly in flank, crumbling it in an instant, capturing a large portion of the First Tennessee, together with General Archer, and sweeping the entire brigade into the field on the other side of the stream.

At this moment the battle was waxing hot between Davis's Confederate brigade and Cutler's by the railroad. Davis was advancing through the field, sending the Fifty-fifth North Carolina north of the railroad, which attacked the flank of the two regiments which Reynolds had placed north of the excavation. Three Mississippi regiments were between the railroad and the turnpike.

General Wadsworth gave an order for Cutler to fall back. The two regiments north of the railroad obeyed, and retired towards the town, but the order did not reach the other regiments of the brigade by McPherson's house. Lieutenant Colonel Miller, commanding the One Hundred and Forty-seventh New York, received it, but before he could issue it fell insensible. Major Harney, who succeeded to the command, knew nothing of it. The Mississippians were coming through the railroad excavation east of Willoughby Run.

The One Hundred and Forty-seventh New York, left alone by the railroad, ignorant of any order to fall back, still continued the contest till more than one half were killed or wounded, when the order came again for them to fall back.

In the field between the railroad and the turnpike is Hall's battery, in great danger at this moment, for the Mississippians are streaming along the railroad to gain its rear.[15]

"Take your guns to the rear and open fire upon them," is Hall's command to Lieutenant Ulmer, who starts with two pieces, gains a new position, but before he can fire all the horses of one piece are shot down, but the men dragged the gun to the rear. The other pieces, one by one, are sent to the rear, except the last, which Hall is obliged to leave, the Confederates shooting all the horses.

The Fourteenth and Ninety-fifth New York are by McPherson's house, facing west, but they fall back, change front and face north, having no intention of abandoning their position. The Sixth Wisconsin, belonging to Meredith's brigade, is in their rear towards the seminary. Doubleday sends it north, and it comes in on the right of the other two regiments. The Mississippians also change front and run into the railroad excavation.

Colonel Fowler, of the Fourteenth New York, had been placed in command of three regiments by General Doubleday. The regiments are by the turnpike fence; a sheet of flame bursts from their muskets. The Union men tear down the fence and rush towards the excavation. Men drop, but others go on. Adjutant Brooks and a portion of the Sixth Wisconsin rush to the eastern end of the excavation, and fire a volley through the cut upon the Mississippians, who find themselves in a trap, with a fire rained upon them and the eastern end closed. They throw down their guns and surrender, while the remainder of Davis's brigade retreats to Willoughby Run. At this moment Wadsworth, who has retired with the other regiments towards Gettysburg, is coming back to re-establish his line.[16]

This the contest of the morning, in which the advantage has been on the side of the Union troops. In the charge the Ninety-seventh New

York lost one hundred and sixty men.

It was nearly eleven o'clock, and for a time there was a lull — the calmness which precedes a fiercer contest — the period of preparation.

Looking down the Emmitsburg Road we see the other two divisions of the First Corps — Rowley's and Robinson's — with the artillery, turning from the road near the house of Mr. Codori, and moving towards the seminary. Not far behind them is General Howard and his staff, who see the battle cloud rising above the green foliage. The general turns to the right, rides to the cemetery, where the white marble head-stones crown the apex of the hill east of the town, and sweeps the landscape with his glass, noting how commanding the situation. To his right, not far away, is Culp's Hill. In the east, down the Baltimore Pike, is Wolf's Hill. Cannon planted in the cemetery and north of it can be made to sweep a large portion of the circle.

"This seems to be a good position, colonel," he remarked to Colonel Mysenburg.[17]

"It is the only position," was the reply.

The topographical advantages were plain. It is no reflection upon Buford or Reynolds that they did not select it. Buford was ordered to hold the town. He bivouacked in the proper place to carry out his orders, and was attacked while there, and Reynolds came to his support. There had been no selection of a place.

General Howard rode through the town. Leaving his horse he climbed a stairway to the observatory of Pennsylvania College, spread out his map and examined it. An officer came galloping down the street with the sad and disheartening information that General Reynolds was wounded. Soon he was informed that Reynolds was dead, and that the command devolved upon him. In a moment he was invested with the command of the right wing of the army, with the responsibility of conducting a battle already begun.

For the remainder of the day General Doubleday commanded the First Corps, and General Schurz the Eleventh.

At eleven o'clock Doubleday was placing Rowley and Robinson in position on Seminary Ridge. Barlow's division of the Eleventh Corps was still far down the Emmitsburg Road — its way blocked by the wagons of the First Corps. Steinwehr's and Schurz's division were nearer, approaching by the Taneytown Road.

General Howard directed Steinwehr to take possession of Cemetery Hill, while Schurz passed through the town and marched northeast along the road to Mummasburg, deploying in the fields.

Leaving the scenes of Gettysburg for the moment and going over the Chambersburg Turnpike, we find General Lee at Cashtown. He has been riding with General Longstreet. They have heard the cannonade, and General Lee hastens over the hills and reaches General Anderson, who is at Cashtown. The firing is deep and heavy from the Confederate batteries at Herr's Tavern and Hall's Second Maine Battery. They can hear the rolls of musketry.[18] General Lee is depressed in spirits. These his words: "I cannot think what has become of Stuart. I ought to have heard from him long before now. He may have met with disaster, but I hope not. In the absence of reports from him I am in ignorance as to what we have in front of us here. It may be the whole Federal army, or it may be only a detachment. If it is the whole Federal force, we must fight a battle here. If we do not gain a victory, those defiles and gorges through which we passed this morning will shelter us from disaster." He rides on towards the scene of conflict.

It was General Howard's intention to post the Eleventh Corps on Oak Hill, the high elevation north of the railroad, the extension of Seminary Ridge, crowned with oaks; but Buford's cavalry videttes came riding in from the north with the startling information that the Confederates in great force were advancing on the Carlisle Road. Howard had supposed the only Confederates before him were those of Hill's corps; this new force must be the advance of Ewell. It was reported that the Twelfth Corps was only five miles distant at Two Taverns, and word was sent to inform General Slocum of the situation of affairs, also to General Sickles, in the direction of Emmitsburg.[19]

At two o'clock in the afternoon the Union troops at Gettysburg were arranged with the

First Corps west of the town, and the Eleventh Corps north of it, with the exception of Steinwehr's division, which was on Cemetery Hill. The nearest troops — those which could be called upon by General Howard — were the Twelfth Corps, five miles distant, in position to come up and form on the right of the Eleventh Corps.

Beginning southwest of the seminary, just beyond where Reynolds fell, at the left of the First Corps, we find Biddle's brigade of Rowley's division in the smooth field south of the grove.

General Meredith, of the "Iron Brigade," has been wounded, and Colonel Morrow commands it. The troops stand where they won their success of the morning — in the woods. From the woods to the turnpike the ground is occupied by Stone's brigade of Rowley's division. It has an angle to defend, the line turning east. Reynolds's First New York Battery is stationed with its guns pointing north. Cutler's brigade is on the ground which it occupied in the morning with Stuart's battery, the Fourth United States.

Crossing the railroad, we come to the Eleventh Pennsylvania, Paul's brigade, the first north of the railroad; then Baxter's brigade of Robinson's division, in a narrow lane, screened by a low wall and a thicket of small oaks. The troops face west, looking over a wheat field sloping gently towards the west.

Paul's brigade is in rear of Baxter's; the

Ninety-fourth New York Regiment on the left, with the Sixteenth Maine facing west; the One Hundred and Fourth New York and the Thirteenth Massachusetts face north, looking up a lane leading to the house of Mr. McLain and his great red barn. Stevens's Fifth Maine Battery is in reserve by the seminary. This completes the formation of the First Corps.

The Eleventh Corps did not arrive upon the field till past noon, and there was little time to arrange it. It was at a right angle with the First Corps. Walking east from the ridge, descending the hill, we find a gap of a quarter of a mile between the Thirteenth Massachusetts and Dilger's Eleventh Ohio Battery. Its intrepid commander wears buckskin breeches, and the soldiers have nicknamed him "Leather Breeches." They admire the skill with which he handles his gun.

There is a wide gap between the two corps at a point where the line turns the angle. Beyond Dilger is Wheeler's Thirteenth New York Battery and Von Amsberg's brigade, holding the ground to the Carlisle Road. Crossing this, we come to Kryzanowski's brigade and Heckman's battery. The two brigades compose Schimmelpfennig's division.

In the fields south of Blocher's house we find Ames's brigade of Barlow's division, with Wilkeson's battery (G, Fourth United States), on a knoll, two of his guns pointing northwest, towards Blocher's house, two northeast, across

Rock Creek, towards the house of Mr. Benner. Two cannon, under Lieutenant Merkle, have been stationed by the Almshouse, nearer the town.

Von Gilsa's brigade is on the extreme right, along Rock Creek.

The sharp action of the morning made the Confederates cautious. Hill knew that Ewell, with two divisions, was rapidly advancing from Carlisle, and waited his arrival before renewing the attack, but placed his troops in position. Going over to Herr's Tavern, where the artillery is planted, and walking south into a beautiful grove, we find, at two o'clock, Heth's division — Brockenborough's and Pettigrew's brigades, with what is left of Archer's and Davis's.

Along the turnpike and in the fields is Pender's division — Thomas's brigade on the north side; McGowan, Lane, and Scales, south. Attached to the two divisions are seventeen batteries — sixty-eighty guns — a large portion of which are placed along the ridge on both sides of the turnpike. Passing through the fields northeast, crossing Rock Creek, we come to Brander's battery; beyond it, the right of Iverson's North Carolina brigade, then O'Neal's Alabama brigade on the summit of Oak Hill. Eastward, extending down into the fields, is Dole's Georgia brigade. Carter's battery comes down through the woods and takes a commanding position on Oak Hill, whence it can rain its missiles upon every part of the Union line — upon the First

Corps, upon Dilger's and Wheeler's batteries, upon Van Amsberg, or even upon Barlow's division. In reserve, behind O'Neal's and Dole's, are Daniel's and Ramseur's brigades. Going east, across Rock Creek, we see Early's division — Gordon's brigade — between the creek and the Harrisburg Road, with three batteries across the road; Hays's and Hoke's brigades deployed in the second line, facing southwest, to envelop Barlow. Johnson's division of Ewell's corps is advancing along the Harrisburg Road, and will arrive before the close of the battle.

It was to be an unequal contest, for the Confederates greatly outnumbered the Union troops, and had the advantage of position.

General Howard rode along the lines at two o'clock. He did not know the danger that threatened his right flank, for Gordon's, Hays's, and Hoke's brigades had not yet appeared. He hoped to hold his position till the Third Corps arrived, not knowing that, through misconception and misunderstanding, it was at that moment ten miles from the scene of conflict. Again he sent a messenger to Slocum, only five miles distant, to come up with the Twelfth Corps and form on his right and assume command, but Slocum did not come.

If Slocum had advanced when Howard sent his first message, quite likely the result of the first day's contest would have been different from what it was.

The Confederate batteries once more opened

fire, concentrating it mainly upon the First Corps and Dilger's and Wheeler's batteries.

There was a gap between Ewell and Hill, and Ewell directed Iverson, Ramseur, and Daniel to march southwest, to bring the two corps nearer together. They crossed the Mummasburg Road, then turned southeast.

The mower had not yet swept the green fields, and the tall grass was waving in its beauty. The Confederate skirmishers crept through it, opening a galling fire upon the Union troops, who saw only puffs of smoke rising above the grass.

The movement of Rodes's troops induced Cutler to change front. He was south of the railroad, facing west, but swung his line to face the north, bringing it into position to send an enfilading fire upon Iverson, who was sweeping round to the west, while O'Neal was advancing directly south. The skirmishers were sheltered by the great red barn of Mr. McLain. They fired from the barn windows, from the fences and sheds, from beneath the apple and peach trees in the garden. It was a threatening cloud of Confederates which pressed down into the gap between the First and Eleventh Corps. Dole intended to drive in a wedge which would break the Union line. Dilger and Wheeler had been sending their shells to the summit of Oak Hill, but now they wheeled and poured a destructive storm upon Dole.

In front of the lane, towards the barn, are the

Thirteenth Massachusetts and One Hundred and Fourth New York, of Paul's brigade. They are in a grove of oaks south of the Mummasburg Road, holding the right of the First Corps. The barn is riddled by their firing. Thick and fast the bullets fly through the garden; equally plenteous are they raining upon the Thirteenth Massachusetts, which charges towards the barn, Sergeant Morris carrying the colors. Suddenly he leaps into the air and falls dead, with his hands grasping the staff.

The concentrated fire upon the Confederates under Dole compels him to fall back.

Iverson's brigade of North Carolinians have been creeping through the tall grass, firing, dropping upon the ground to reload, thus screening themselves from the fire of Baxter's brigade, sheltered by the scrubby oaks. There comes a lightning flash from beneath the green foliage, and the men of North Carolina go down as if smitten by a thunderbolt; not all by the fire of Baxter, but in part by a volley from Cutler's brigade across the railroad.

"Let us capture them!" is the cry that runs along the lines. "Forward, Twelfth!" is the word of command from Adjutant Wherum. Over the wall leaps the Twelfth Massachusetts, through the shrubbery dashes the Eighty-eighth Pennsylvania and the other regiments — each soldier instinctively seeing that it is the right thing to be done — all rushing down upon the astonished Confederates.

"The enemy charged," says Iverson, "in over-whelming force, and captured nearly all that were left unhurt of the three regiments of my brigade. When I saw white handkerchiefs raised and my line of battle still lying down, in position, I characterized the surrender as disgraceful; but when afterwards I found that five hundred of my men were left lying dead and wounded, and in a line as straight as a dress parade, I exonerated the survivors, and claim that they nobly fought and died, without a man running to the rear. No greater gallantry or heroism during the war. . . . The fighting ceased on my part."[20]

"The dead lay in a distinctly marked line of battle," are the words of General Rodes.[21]

It was nearly three o'clock, and the battle was becoming more intense.

"At 3:45," says General Howard, "Generals Doubleday and Wadsworth besought me for reinforcements. I directed General Schurz, if he could spare a regiment or more, to send it to reinforce General Wadsworth, and several times sent urgent requests to General Slocum to come to my assistance. To every application for reinforcements I replied, 'Hold out if possible a while longer, for I am expecting General Slocum every moment.' . . . About 4 P.M. I dispatched Major Howard, my aide, to General Slocum to inform him of the state of affairs, and request him to send one of his divisions to the left and the other to the right of Gettysburg. He met the general on the Baltimore Pike, about a mile from

Gettysburg, who replied that he had already ordered a division to the right, and that he would send another to cover the left, as requested, but that he did not wish to come up to the front and take the responsibility of that fight. In justice to General Slocum, I desire to say that he afterwards expressed the opinion that it was against the wish of the commanding general to bring on a general engagement at that point."[22]

The Twelfth Corps had arrived at Two Taverns during the forenoon, after a march from Littlestown in the early morning. The cannonade and musketry could be distinctly heard by the troops as they rested in the fields around Two Taverns. A general engagement had begun, inaugurated by General Reynolds, commanding the left wing of the army, who had been killed. General Slocum outranked General Howard, and did not wish to assume any responsibility.

General Slocum's course has been open to much criticism, but he claimed that General Meade did not desire to have a battle at Gettysburg.

Let us look at affairs as they were at three o'clock on the right of the Union line. A part of the Seventeenth Connecticut had been sent across Rock Creek as skirmishers, but were being driven back by Early's advancing line of battle. The only battery which could be spared on the Union side for the right of the line was G, Fourth United States, commanded by Lieutenant Wilkeson, who had placed four of his light 12-pounders on a knoll overlooking a wide reach of fields on both sides of Rock Creek, and two pieces nearer the town, by the Almshouse, under Lieutenant Merkle. The Seventeenth Connecticut, and Twenty-fifth, Seventy-fifth, and One Hundred and Seventh Ohio, constituted the brigade of General Ames, assigned to hold this important position, with no reserve that could be called upon in the hour of need. Von Gilsa, along Rock Creek, must hold the flank. The artillery duel began, between Wilkeson, with four pieces, and twelve guns on the part of the Confederates.

Wilkeson was supported by the Seventeenth Connecticut Regiment.

It was a trying situation for the cannoneers of the Union battery. Their commander, to encourage them, to inspire them with his own lofty spirit, sat upon his horse, a conspicuous figure, calmly directing the fire of the pieces. He rode from piece to piece, his horse upon the walk. Shells were bursting amid the guns; shot from rifled cannon cut the air or ploughed the ground, from cannon not half a mile away, upon a hill much higher than that which he occupied. This young lieutenant bore an honored name — Bayard Wilkeson — a family name, given him in part, also, by his parents out of their admiration for the great Chevalier of France, the knight of other days, whose character was without a stain, whose life was above reproach. This self-possessed lieutenant from New York, animated by an unquenchable patriotism, became a soldier at sixteen, received his commission when he was but seventeen, and was not then nineteen years of age. His first battle was Fredericksburg. For six months he had been commander — his captain engaged elsewhere. So admirable the discipline and efficient the battery under the instruction of this boy-lieutenant that it had been accorded the post of honor — the right of the line. It is a brave spirit that can look out composedly upon the scene in a contest so unequal, but his guns are fired with precision and effect. A rifled cannon shot strikes his right leg, crushing the bones and mangling the flesh. His soldiers lay him upon the ground. With composure he ties his handkerchief around it, twists it into a tourniquet to stop the flow of blood, then with his own hand and knife severs the cords and tendons, and, sitting there, tells his cannoneers to go on with their fire — a bravery unsurpassed even by that of the Chevalier of France beneath the walls of Brescia, in Italy, who said to his soldiers, when wounded, "Let me lie with my face to the enemy, for I never yet have learned to turn my back upon the foe." Faint and thirsty, he sends a soldier with his canteen to fill it at the Almshouse well. When the man returns, a wounded infantryman whose life is ebbing away, beholding the canteen, exclaims, "Oh that I could have but a swallow!" Like Sir Philip Sidney, author of the "Arcadia," upon the field of Zutphen, who said to a wounded soldier by his side, "Drink, comrade, your necessities are greater than mine," so Bayard Wilkeson, with like unselfishness, courtesy, and benevolence, replies, "Drink, comrade; I can wait." In the consuming thirst and fever of approaching death the infantryman drains the canteen of its contents. When it was seen that the line must retire, Wilkeson allowed himself to be carried to the Almshouse hospital, which, a few minutes later, was within the advancing lines of the Confederates, and where, during the night, for want of attention, he died. Dead — but his heroism, sense of duty, responsibility to obligation, devotion, and loyalty remain; and by the majesty of his death he shall be evermore an inspiration to those who love the country which he died to save.[23]

The weak point in the Union line was the angle between the First and Eleventh Corps — the wide gap, with only Dilger's battery to hold it. General Howard, possibly from want of information in regard to Ewell's force and position, ordered Schimmelpfennig to advance. The movement enabled Ewell's batteries on Oak Hill to send down a destructive enfilading fire, which compelled the line to fall back. It was rallied in part. At this moment Early advanced, with Gordon's brigade on the right, Hays in the centre, Hoke on the left, with Smith in reserve — moving down to Rock Creek, the soldiers plashing through it on the flank of Von Gilsa by the York Road. It was like the drawing of a seine by fishermen. At the same moment Dole was pushing into the gap between the First and Eleventh Corps. The Union line was forced back. Barlow, commanding a division, was wounded and carried from the field. By the Almshouse the battle was renewed, but the Eleventh Corps was rapidly crumbling. The falling back of the left of the Eleventh Corps compelled Robinson, on the right of the First, to change position. Going down the line of the First Corps, we see Meredith's division still holding the ground of the morning, reduced by losses to less than one thousand. Meredith and Rowley have held Heth's division at bay, but now they must meet the onset of Pender's fresh brigades. Meredith is in the woods, where he has been through the day; Rowley in the field by McPherson's. The Confederates advance boldly, but are met by a terrific fire. Pender and Scales, commanding a brigade, are both wounded, and the Confederate line retreats in disorder. Perrin's Confederate brigade falls upon Biddle's, which is forced back towards the seminary, and Meredith, with both flanks exposed, is compelled to abandon the ground which has been held since morning. Meredith is wounded, and Colonel Morrow succeeds to the command. In perfect order, with steady ranks, the two divisions fall back to the seminary ridge, where a breastwork of rails has been erected, and where the troops face once more to the west, confronting the Confederates, and deliver a fire, which holds Daniel's Confederates in check; while Doubleday's artillery, planted along the ridge by the seminary, cuts great gaps in Scales's brigade of Pender's division. Scales and Pender are both wounded. Scales's men rush up almost to the muzzles of the cannon, but are swept back by the remorseless fire. Every field officer of the Confederate brigade but one is wounded.

Southward Buford's men, who have been on the field since daylight, leap from their saddles, deploy as infantry, and deliver a fire which prevents the Confederates from closing upon Doubleday's flank.

Cutler halts behind the railroad embankment in the field between Seminary Ridge and the town, and holds Rodes in check, enabling the Union artillery to get across the field south of the town.

The One Hundred and Forty-ninth Pennsylvania and Baxter's brigade were still on the ridge, holding out so stubbornly that Hill advanced cautiously.

Hall's battery, moving towards the town, unlimbered and sent its shells along the street upon the advancing Confederates. But the conflict was over. General Howard had seen the crumbling of the Eleventh Corps, and had ordered the retreat. Down from the Almshouse, from the Carlisle Road, from the York Road, came the men of the Eleventh Corps, those of Barlow's division loading and firing on their retreat.

This is the testimony of A. P. Hill: "A Yankee color bearer floated his standard in the field, and the regiment fought around it; and when at last it was obliged to retreat, the color bearer, last of all, turning round now and then to shake his fist in the face of the advancing rebels, I was sorry when I saw him meet his doom."[24]

Three color bearers of the Nineteenth Indiana, one after the other, were shot. The sergeant major, Asa Blanchard, ran and seized the flag when the third man fell, waved it, and cried, "Rally, boys!" The next moment he fell. His comrades stopped to carry him. "Don't stop for me," he cried; "don't let them have the flag. Tell mother I never faltered." They were his parting words to his comrades who saved the flag.

Five color bearers of the Twenty-fourth Michigan were shot. Colonel Morrow seized the flag, but was wounded. A soldier grasped it, but fell mortally wounded.

General Paul was made totally blind for life by a bullet which passed through his eyes. General Robinson had two horses shot beneath him.

Down the Chambersburg, down the Carlisle, the Mummasburg, and Harrisburg roads into the town pressed the retreating troops. It was like a spring freshet from a vast area of country pouring through a narrow gorge — divisions, brigades, regiments — infantry, artillery, and cavalry — were in confusion. They streamed through the fields, climbed the fences, the Confederates rushing on to capture them. The First

Corps retired partly across the meadow south of the town, losing but few prisoners; but north of the town the Eleventh Corps, blocked by the houses, pressed by Early's division, suffered great loss.

Some of Barlow's men turned about and deliberately fired into the faces of the enemy, refusing to surrender, and we were shot down by men who admired their bravery.

"I never have seen," said General Gordon, "more desperate fighting than around the Almshouse, between my brigade and Barlow's, of the Eleventh Corps."

General Barlow fell and was taken prisoner. Among those who sought shelter in the houses was Colonel Wheelock, of the Ninety-seventh New York, a large man, who could not make his way through the crowd, and who would have disdained to run had he been able to do so. He entered the house of Mr. Shead, followed by Confederate soldiers and an officer who demanded his sword.[25] "I'll not surrender my sword to a rebel," was the reply. "Surrender your sword, or I will shoot you." "Shoot! I'll not surrender it," again the defiant reply from Wheelock, who opened his vest, waiting for the fatal shot. A girl sprang between them — Miss Carrie Shead — who seized the sword, bore it away, and secreted it. His sword safe, Colonel Wheelock became a submissive prisoner. With the three thousand other prisoners he was taken outside the town, but during the night managed to escape, returning to Gettysburg upon the retirement of the Confederates, and regained his sword.

General Schimmelpfennig, whom his soldiers greatly loved, and whom they familiarly called Schimmel, remained upon the field to the last. His horse was shot, and the Confederates of Dole's division were close upon him. He ran into the woodshed of Mr. Garloch, jumped behind some barrels, and drew sticks of wood over him. The Confederates looked in, but did not see him. Three nights and two days he remained. Mrs. Garloch saw him, and her little boy dropped bread behind the barrels. The Confederates were frequently in the shed. When, at last, on Saturday, he heard the Union drumbeat in the street, he emerged from his hiding place and returned to his brigade.

Out near the battle line of the Eleventh Corps, in an enclosed lot near Pennsylvania College, lay a Union soldier. No one was near him; he heard no footstep coming to his relief. If he uttered a cry of pain, a wail of agony, or call for help, there was no one to hasten to his assistance. For him there was but one solace — to gaze once more upon those who were dearest, but who were far away. When the battle was ended, the Confederates departed, the people of Gettysburg discovered the prostrate form, motionless evermore, the clinched fingers holding the photograph of his wife and three children. His last fading sight of things earthly was of their fair faces; his last thoughts were of them. The good people buried him where he fell. They rephotographed the group and sent the picture far and wide throughout the North. It was recognized in Cattaraugus County, New York, as the wife and children of a soldier of the One Hundred and Fifty-fourth New York Regiment of Costar's brigade — one of the men who went down through Gettysburg upon the run, and out upon the York Road, at the last moment of the struggle.

Half-past four o'clock came, the battle was decided, and what was left of the First and Eleventh Corps were gathered on Cemetery Hill — the Eleventh Corps north of the turnpike, the First Corps south of it.

General Hancock, commander of the Second Corps, was riding up the Baltimore Pike, with instructions from General Meade to take command of the troops at Gettysburg. He was the junior of Howard in rank. "General Meade undoubtedly supposed that I was your senior, but you outrank me," said Hancock.[26]

"It is no time to talk about rank. I shall most cheerfully obey your instructions, and do all in my power to cooperate with you," Howard replied, taking charge of the troops north of the turnpike, Hancock south of it, and in a few moments they had a gleaming line of bayonets in position.

It was five o'clock — the sun yet two hours in the heavens. General Lee and General Longstreet were by the Theological Seminary, gazing upon the scene, having just arrived upon the field.

"I think that we will attack them upon the heights tomorrow morning," said General Lee.[27]

"Will not that be a departure from the plan as proposed before we left Fredericksburg?" suggested Longstreet.

"If the enemy is there tomorrow we must attack him."

"But if he is there it will be because he is anxious that we should attack him — a good reason, in my judgment, for not doing so. Let us move by our right to Meade's left, and put our army between him and Washington, threatening his left and rear, and thus force him to attack us in such position as we may select. His weak point is his left. I think we should move around it, threaten by the maneuver, and attack if we determine upon a battle. The country is admirably adapted for a defensive battle, and we shall surely repulse Meade by a crushing loss if we take the position and force him to attack us. Even if we attack the heights before us and drive him out, we shall be so badly crippled that we shall not be able to reap the fruits of victory. The heights of Gettysburg are in themselves of no more importance than the ground upon which we stand. Meade's army, and not its position, is our objective."

General Lee, before starting upon the campaign, had a fixed determination to reach a position of his own choosing, and await an attack;

but the two armies had come in collision, and the Confederates had already won a victory — another in the long list that had crowned the arms of his troops, who regarded themselves as invincible, and who were eager to attack in the morning. Their blood was up, and so was that of General Lee.

"He seemed under a subdued excitement, which occasionally took possession of him when the hunt was up and threatened his superb equipoise," are the words of Longstreet.[28]

"The enemy is in position, and I am going to whip them or they are going to whip me."[29]

At the hour of five in the afternoon I was twenty miles away. Through the day I had been riding with General Gregg's division of cavalry. At three o'clock we were at Hanover Junction, twenty-five miles from the battlefield, upon the extreme right of the Union army. We had removed the saddles from our horses for a brief halt, when the booming of cannon came upon us from the west. Leaving the cavalry, I rode towards it, but soon found that it was not the cannonade of the conflict at Gettysburg, but at Hanover, between Kilpatrick's cavalry and the Confederate cavalry under Stuart. I arrived in season to see its close.

General Stuart had captured four hundred prisoners and gathered two hundred wagons, which hindered him; but he would not abandon the wagons. He bivouacked halfway between Westminster and Littlestown. His scouts came in during the evening of June 30 with the information that the Union cavalry was at Littlestown — Kilpatrick's two brigades.

General Stuart, instead of marching to Littlestown, as he had intended, decided to get away from the Union cavalry by going northeast. Chambliss's brigade was in advance. Fitzhugh Lee moved along the left flank to guard the train, while Hampton covered the rear. Chambliss approached Hanover, but discovered a column of Union troops entering the town — Kilpatrick's division. At Aldie that officer commanded a brigade, but now he was in command of a division — Farnsworth's and Custer's brigades. Farnsworth was moving quietly into Hanover, with Custer west of him.

Stuart ordered Chambliss to charge upon the Union troops, and almost the first intimation Farnsworth had of the presence of the Confederates was the yelling of Chambliss's men as they thundered along the turnpike, charging upon the rear guard, scattering it, and capturing several soldiers and ambulances. The Fifth New York, under Major Hammond, turned upon the Confederates and put them to flight. Kilpatrick hastened up, formed his line, and sent word to Custer.

Stuart planted his artillery and opened fire. The Second North Carolina advanced, but was repulsed, and its commander, Colonel Payn, taken prisoner. Stuart had no desire to fight a battle. He was anxious rather to avoid one. He must join Lee, and his only aim was to hold Kilpatrick in check till the long train of wagons could glide by. Fitzhugh Lee joined him, and the artillery duel went on. Hampton arrived. Stuart was stronger than Kilpatrick, but the skirmishing went on till sunset — charges and countercharges around and through the town. Stuart, having secured the passage of his train, moved towards York, in search of General Early.

The Union cavalry bivouacked near the town. Stuart made an all-night march to get beyond the reach of Kilpatrick. Horses and men were worn down. Whole regiments fell asleep, the horses stumbled, bringing the riders to the ground. No rest for the horses or men was allowed till they reached Carlisle in the afternoon of July 2, having ridden one hundred and twenty-five miles without rest. He was then thirty miles north of Gettysburg.

Thus the first day of July closed upon one of the hardest fought engagements of the war, with the Confederate army well concentrated and elated with victory, the Union army yet widely scattered, and dispirited by the defeat of two corps with heavy loss.

# Chapter IV

# *Little Round Top*

*When night* closed over the scene of the first day's engagement at Gettysburg, the various corps of the Union army were widely separated. The rallied brigades of the First Corps were in the cemetery and the field immediately before it towards the town — ground now included in the National Cemetery. What was left of the Eleventh Corps was on the north side of the turnpike. The Twelfth Corps, under Slocum, had crossed Rock Creek, turned to the right through the pastures, and taken position in the woods on Culp's Hill. The Second Corps was on the march from Uniontown, and arrived during the evening. The Third Corps was on its way from Emmitsburg, but did not all arrive till eight o'clock the next morning. The Fifth Corps was at Bonnaughtown, five miles away in the direction of Hanover, while the Sixth Corps was twenty-eight miles distant.

It was one o'clock in the morning of July 2 when General Meade, who on Sunday had accepted the great trust laid upon him by President Lincoln, came up the Taneytown Road, and dismounted from his horse by the home of Mrs. Leister. He was worn down with want of sleep, with constant thinking as to what ought to be done. He had thought of selecting Pike Creek, near Taneytown, as a line of defense, and General Warren, of the Engineer Corps, had been examining the ground, while General Humphreys had been surveying the country in the direction of Emmitsburg. The battle already fought had not been anticipated. The army had already met with a defeat. What should he do? Should he make a stand at Gettysburg, or fall back to Pipe Creek? General Hancock had informed him that the position to which the First and Eleventh Corps had retreated was a strong one. He had come to see. With General Howard he rode along the lines. The moon was shining, and he could dimly see the general features of the country — that Culp's Hill was covered with trees, that its northern side was sharp and steep, that Cemetery Hill commanded a wide sweep of country, that there was a low ridge running southeast towards Little Round Top, two miles from the cemetery. Sitting upon his horse amid the white headstones, he could look over the houses in the town and see the seminary ridge, where the First Corps had fought so stubbornly, and the level fields northward, where the Eleventh Corps had stood. He could trace the dark line of forest extending southward from the seminary, and see that the entire region would be under the sweep of artillery placed in the cemetery and north of it, or along the ridge. It was a place where possibly a battle might be successfully fought. He directed General Warren and General Slocum to examine the ground in front of Culp's Hill with a view of attacking Lee in that direction, and that breastworks should be constructed. From two o'clock till morning the soldiers on Culp's Hill, on Cemetery Hill, and in the grove of oaks on the farm of Mr. Zeigler, south of the cemetery, were at work with axes and shovels. General Slocum informed General Meade that the ground in front of Culp's Hill was not favorable for an attack upon the Confederates, and that it would be far better to fight a defensive battle.

General Lee was up very early in the morning, and was eating his breakfast in his tent north of the seminary, near a small stone house, before the sun appeared. General Longstreet came to see him, riding in from Cashtown, and tried to dissuade him from making an attack upon the Union army; but General Lee had made up his mind to do so, and they talked of what would be the probable result. General Hill came, and also General Heth, who was wounded in the head the day before, and who had a handkerchief bandaged around it. Up in a tree nearby was Lieutenant Colonel Freemantle, of the British Army, looking across the fields with his glass at the Union position. With him were a Prussian and an Austrian officer. General Lee thought of having General Ewell begin the battle by attacking the Union troops at Culp's Hill. He sent Colonel Venable to reconnoiter the ground, and then himself rode across the fields where the Eleventh Corps had fought, to take a look at the position. It was nine o'clock when he got back to his headquarters, and it was eleven before he had made up his mind just what to do.

"It will not do to have Ewell open the attack. I have decided that you must make it on the extreme right," he said to Longstreet.[1]

General Pickett's division of Longstreet's corps was still near Chambersburg, guarding the great train of wagons, and General Law's brigade was out on picket duty. Law was sent for, but the village clocks were striking twelve before he was in from the picket line.

"The troops must make the movement cautiously, under cover of the woods, so as not to be seen by the enemy," were the instructions of Lee.[2] He could see from his headquarters that a Union signal officer was on Little Round Top waving his flags to another by Meade's headquarters. So, on the Confederate side, the forenoon passed, only that the picket lines of the two armies in the wheat fields and along the fences, from orchard and meadow, were exchanging shots, and now and then a Confederate cannon sent a shot whirring over the town, followed by answering shots from the Union cannon among the white headstones in the cemetery.

The sun was just rising when I mounted my horse at Hanover, twelve miles away. I rode towards Gettysburg, passing a long train of wagons and many soldiers of the Fifth Corps, who had dropped, weary and exhausted, by the roadside. The troops of the corps were east of Rock Creek, where they had been halted by General Meade, in anticipation of his attacking Lee; but he having determined to fight a defensive battle, they filed southward through the fields, crossed the creek, turned into a pasture, and threw themselves wearily upon the ground. I rode up the Baltimore Turnpike, with the Twelfth Corps on my right hand, partly hidden from view by the woods, passed the tollgate, from which the tollman had fled, reached the summit of the hill where the soldiers of the Eleventh Corps, on my right, were lying down, and those of the First Corps, on my left, were crouching behind a stone wall. On both sides the artillerymen had thrown up breastworks to shield themselves in part. Dismounting from my horse, I climbed the stairs of the arched gateway of the cemetery and beheld the grand panorama of the field where yesterday's battle had been fought, the town, with its houses of red brick, its spires and steeples, the white walls of Pennsylvania College north of the town — Almshouse beyond, where Barlow's division had fought and left its line of dead. With my glass I could see the prostrate forms lying where they fell. A yellow flag was flying above the cupola of the Theological Seminary, which had been taken for a hospital. The fields in the distance by Herr's

Tavern, where the Confederate cannon had been planted, were dotted with white tents, trains of wagons were winding here and there, and horsemen were riding rapidly. Southward were fields and woodlands and farmhouses — the ground where the great battle was to be fought. Eastward was Culp's Hill; upon its western face the soldiers were at work with picks and shovels throwing up a breastwork, behind which stood a Union battery — the Fifth Maine. We shall see it again by-and-by. Immediately around, upon Cemetery Hill, cannon were thickly planted, some of them pointing north, others west, and others southwest. A short distance southward, across the Taneytown Road, was the grove on the farm of Mr. Zeigler. On the Emmitsburg Road was the brick house of Mr. Codori, with a large barn. Beyond, upon the west side of the road, was the house of Peter Rogers, and still farther away the farmhouse of Mr. Sherfy, and an orchard of peach trees, whence a crossroad ran eastward towards Little Round Top. Eastward of the peach trees, across the green fields, a quarter of a mile, was the house and barn of Mr. Trostle. I could see cannon along the Emmitsburg Road pointing westward, and regiments were lying down by the house of Mr. Codori and beyond it — the troops of the Third Corps, resting themselves after their hard march from Emmitsburg, kindling fires and cooking coffee. By the house of Mr. Leister, on the Taneytown Road, the headquarters flag of

General Meade was waving. The Second Corps was on the ridge west of it. Long lines of white-topped wagons dotted the landscape eastward.

Descending from the gateway, I mounted my horse to ride into Gettysburg, and came to a soldier crouching behind a picket fence.

"Halt! Where are you going?" he said.

"Into Gettysburg."

"Into Gettysburg! Do you know where you are? I am on the picket line. Do you see that brick house with the window open? That is full of Confederates, and they have been picking us off all the morning, and the quicker you get out of here the better it will be for you."

The house was within pistol shot, and I rode back to the cemetery. General Howard was there; his servant came with his breakfast of cold ham, hard biscuit, and coffee.

"You are just in season," he said.

He had deep religious convictions, and reverently asked God's blessing before eating.

"Lieutenant," he said to an officer, "have a detail of men to take up these gravestones and lay them carefully upon the ground. If they are left standing the cannonballs will knock them to pieces, and send the fragments about our ears. The people of the town can reset them."

He told the story of the first day's engagement, and pointed out the positions of the troops. Looking across the houses, we could see at that moment a column of Confederates on the Chambersburg Road.

"See there! See there, general! Let Osborne open on them with his artillery," shouted Major Charles Howard, of his staff.

"No, the time hasn't come. Don't be in a hurry about it; you will have enough fighting before sunset."

The Confederates were a part of Doles's division changing position. I rode with General Howard along the lines and to the headquarters of General Meade, where a group of officers were consulting the maps which the engineers had hastily sketched.

In the dooryard of Meade's headquarters a signal officer was waving his flag in response to another on Little Round Top.

"Large bodies of Confederate troops moving south," was the message received.

I rode along the line south from Zeigler's Grove towards Mr. Codori's house, on the Emmitsburg Road, near which was Hall's brigade of Gibson's division of the Second Corps, thrown out in advance of the cemetery ridge. A few steps farther brought me to Carr's brigade of Humphreys's division of the Third Corps.

Some of the soldiers — First Massachusetts — were clustered round the door of a small house on the west side of the road eating delicious bread, piping hot, just baked. When Carr's brigade arrived, just before daylight, they saw a light in the house of Peter Rogers. Going to the door and looking in, they saw two tallow candles on the mantle, and a young girl, in her fourteenth year, kneading dough in a tin pan, with several other pans on the floor with dough in them.

"Could you let us have some bread?" asked a soldier.

"Oh yes, if you can wait for it a little. My stove is small, and you know when one is in a hurry bread don't bake fast," said Josephine Miller, who invited them in to wait till the bread was ready. It was an old-fashioned stove, with an oven, but not designed for general cooking.[3]

"I think it must be done now," she said, after a little while, and took out two pans of most palatable bread, and put in two more, breaking the loaves for the soldiers.

"What will you do when the battle begins?" Asked Colonel Baldwin, commanding the First Massachusetts.

"Is there really going to be a battle? Where shall we go?"

"Yes, we shall have a battle right here, and you will either have to go to the rear or down the cellar, if you have one."

"Yes, we have a small cellar. I think we will stay;" and Josephine Miller went on with her baking.

The line which General Sickles had selected was along the Emmitsburg Road, southward to the peach orchard of Mr. Sherfy, thence eastward towards Little Round Top. There has been much controversy as to whether or not General Sickles carried out General Meade's instructions in the selection of the line, and also much discussion whether or not it was the best position. Upon both questions military men have been divided in opinion.

It was past noon, and the Confederates, instead of attacking in the morning, as General Lee had intended the night before, were not yet in position. Had General Lee known the position of the Union army at eight o'clock in the morning, he doubtless would have attacked with great vigor; but, for various reasons, the Confederate generals were slow in getting ready. Under the orders of General Lee, the troops of Longstreet were trying to get down through the woods by Mr. Warfield's, without being seen by the Union signal officer on Little Round Top. Colonel Johnson, of the engineers, was leading them.[4] The column came to a halt, for he had reached an opening where the troops would be seen; Longstreet became impatient. Johnson was carrying out General Lee's orders, which had been issued directly to him by the Confederate commander, and it would be a breach of military etiquette were Longstreet to order him to move on regardless of the Union signal officer; but General Hood had received no orders from General Lee, and Longstreet, therefore, directed him to move into position by the best route, and the column took up its line of march.

"Do you not think it would be well to send a party down into those woods to see what is going on?" was the suggestion of Colonel Berdan, commanding the First Regiment of Union sharpshooters west of the Emmitsburg Road, holding the picket line.[5]

"Yes, and I will send you supports," General Sickles replied.

Colonel Berdan advanced with his men, deployed, and came upon Hood. Instantly there was a sharp rattle of musketry, lasting fifteen minutes, during which time half of the men in the detachment of sharpshooters were killed or wounded. The encounter was so hotly waged by them that it brought Hood to a halt. He did not know just what was before him, and waited to find out, thus delaying the opening of the battle.

It was three o'clock before Hood and McLaws were in position, and before Colonel Alexander, of Longstreet's corps, had his batteries unlimbered in the edge of the woods west and south of the peach orchard. The general plan on the part of Lee was to swing Longstreet, together with R. H. Anderson's division of Hill's corps, against Meade's left flank, and that Ewell at the same time should strike the Twelfth Corps on Culp's Hill. Longstreet frequently dismounted from his horse and walked to positions where he could see the Union line. General Barksdale, commanding the Mississippi brigade, was eager for the battle to begin. He could see a Union battery in the peach orchard, and wanted to capture it.

"I wish you would let me go in, general. I would take it in five minutes," said Barksdale.

"Wait a little; we are all going in presently," said Longstreet.[6]

The men were impatient, and began to pull down a fence in front of them.

"Don't do that; you will draw the enemy's fire," said Longstreet. He was not quite ready. But soon came the word from his lips, "Forward!" and the lines moved on.

The Confederate army was never in better spirits than at that moment, never more confident of success.

General Longstreet saw that Sickles occupied a position easy to be assailed, and placed his batteries in the edge of the woods southwest of the peach orchard on the farm of Mr. Warfield. McLaws's division was to advance directly upon the orchard, while Hood was to move towards Little Round Top. Anderson's division of Hill's corps was to strike the right of Sickles's line by the house where Josephine Miller was baking bread.

General Law's brigade was on the extreme right of Hood's line of battle. Six scouts were sent out to move as rapidly as possible towards Great Round Top and find out the position of the Union army in that direction.[7] They soon brought in a Union prisoner who had a surgeon's certificate, and who said that he belonged to the medical department, that the trains were east of Round Top, and not guarded. One of the scouts came in and reported that there were no Union troops on Round Top. Law hastened to Hood with the information, and protested against attacking in front. This was his reason:

"The great natural strength of the enemy's position in our front rendered the result of a direct attack extremely uncertain; that, if successful, the victory would be purchased at too great a sacrifice of life, and our troops would be in no condition to improve it; that the attack was unnecessary, because they could easily gain the left and rear of the enemy; that it would compel the enemy to change front and abandon his position.

"General Hood called up Captain Hamilton of his staff, and requested me to repeat the protest to him. He directed Hamilton to find Longstreet as soon as possible, to deliver the protest, and say to him that he [Hood] indorsed it fully. Hamilton rode off at once, but in about ten minutes returned, accompanied by one of General Longstreet's staff officers, who said to General Hood in my hearing, 'General Longstreet orders that you begin the attack at once.' Hood turned to me and merely said, 'You hear the order.' I at once moved my brigade to the assault. . . . General Longstreet has since said that he repeatedly advised against a front attack, and suggested a movement by our right flank. He may have thought, after the rejection of this advice by General Lee, that it was useless to press the matter further."

Longstreet had eight brigades, and Anderson five — thirteen in all — with the brigades of

Hill's corps in reserve, which were moving to attack the six brigades of the Third Corps. To understand the battle, we are to keep in mind the uncertainty of General Meade as to the intentions of Lee. From Little Round Top Confederate troops could be seen moving south, while from Cemetery Hill I could see those north of the town moving east. With this uncertainty before him, General Meade was holding the Fifth Corps in reserve not far from his headquarters, that he might use it in any direction. The line of defense which General Meade had selected was along the ridge from the cemetery to Little Round Top, but the Third Corps was not on the ridge; it was in front of it, and made a sharp angle at the peach orchard. General Hunt, commanding the artillery, rode along the line with General Sickles to the peach orchard, and down to Little Round Top. With his quick eye he saw that the peach orchard was quite as high as the ground along the ridge between the position of the Second Corps and Little Round Top; that it would be a position where the Confederates might plant their artillery and pour a destructive fire upon the Union line. For that reason it might be desirable to hold it; but the line there turned a right angle, and that was a disadvantage. This is what General Hunt says in regard to it:

"The salient line proposed by General Sickles, although much longer, afforded excellent positions for our artillery; its occupation would cramp the movements of the enemy, bring us nearer his lines, and afford us facilities for taking the offensive. It was, in my judgment, the better line of the two, provided it were strongly occupied, for it was the only one on the field from which we could have passed from the defensive to the offensive with a prospect of decisive results. But General Meade had not, until the arrival of the Sixth Corps, a sufficient number of troops at his disposal to risk such an extension of his lines; it would have required both the Third and Fifth Corps, and left him without any reserve. Had he known that Lee's attack would be postponed till 4 P.M. he might have occupied the line in the morning; but he did not know this, expected an attack at any moment, and, in view of the vast risks involved, adopted a defensive policy and ordered the occupation of the safe line."[8]

It was at this moment that the troops of Ewell were moving east towards Culp's Hill, upon which the batteries on Cemetery Hill opened fire; it was also the moment of the encounter between sharpshooters and Hood.

General Meade rode down to the peach orchard and examined the line, at the suggestion of General Hunt, who says:

"I was here met by Captain Randolph, the Third Corps chief of artillery, who informed me that he had been ordered to place his batteries on the new line. Seeing Generals Meade and Sickles not far off in conversation, and supposing that General Meade had consented to the occupation, I sent at once to the Reserve for more artillery, and authorized other general officers to draw on the same source."

There were one hundred and eight guns in the Reserve Artillery, which could be summoned for use on any part of the field, in addition to the two hundred and twelve attached to the several corps.

General Sickles had stationed Ward's brigade, with four guns of Smith's New York Battery, on the rocky ridge west of the Devil's Den, to hold the extreme left of his line and the approach to Little Round Top. He had stationed Winslow's New York Battery on the eastern edge of a wheat field east of Rose's house, between Ward's brigade and De Trobriand's brigade, which was located in the woods west of the wheat field with part of Burling's brigade. This brings us to the gap extending from the woods to the peach orchard — quite a distance along the road, where there was not a regiment of infantry. The other regiments of Burling's brigade, together with Graham's brigade and Clark's New Jersey Battery, held the line in the peach orchard facing south towards Rose's house. Humphreys's division of the Third Corps, with several batteries, held the Emmitsburg Road northward to Codori's house. It was too late to make any change in the line, for the Confederate batteries were opening fire, and the battle must begin with the troops as they stood. Lee's army consisted of forty brigades, and eighteen of them were in position to take part in the attack upon the six brigades of the Third Corps, which must look to the Second and Fifth Corps for assistance.

The horses of the Union Reserve Artillery had eaten their oats, the cannoneers were resting beneath the shade of the trees, smoking their pipes and playing cards, when an aide arrived from General Hunt with an order to Colonel McGilvery for more batteries. Hart's Fifteenth New York, Phillips's Fifth Massachusetts, and Bigelow's Ninth Massachusetts went out past Trostle's house; Hart's to take position in the peach orchard, Phillips's and Bigelow's to fill the gap along the road leading eastward from the orchard.

The sun was going down in the western sky — a lovely summer afternoon. The swallows were twittering around the eaves of Mrs. Leister's humble home, unmindful of the coming and going of men on horseback. Fleecy clouds flecked the sky, and a gentle breeze came from the southwest, as yet untainted with nitrous and sulphurous fumes. For an hour there had been a pattering fire, like the first drops which precede a summer shower. Suddenly the Confederate cannon in the woods by Mr. Warfield's opened fire; also those north of Culp's Hill — the artillery of Ewell's corps. The Union batteries were quick to respond. Then came the rattling fire of Stoughton's sharpshooters — the Second Regiment, posted behind a wall and fences — delivered into the faces of Law's Alabama brigade. The sharpshooters held their ground with great pertinacity. "My whole regiment," writes Colonel Sheffield, of the Forty-eighth Alabama, "was brought to the front the third time, only to be driven back."[9]

"In a few seconds one-fourth of my regiment were killed or disabled," is the statement of the colonel of the Forty-fourth Alabama.[10]

When the sharpshooters were compelled to fall back, a portion retreated past the left flank of Ward's brigade, in front of Little Round Top, held by the Fourth Maine. We shall see them again.

Onward through the woods, crossing the brook which trickles south from Mr. Rose's house, past his spring house, where he kept his milk, marched Law's and Robertson's brigades, following the sharpshooters. They were in the woods, where there are large trees and boulders. They began to ascend the slope towards the position held by Ward.

"Don't fire until you can see them plainly," were the instructions of Ward.

The troops of his brigade could hear the rustling of last year's dead leaves as the sharpshooters came streaming in. Smith's four cannon began to flash, and then the battle broke out in all its fury — rolls of musketry, the yells of the Texans of Hood's division, and the cheers of the Union men, the wails of the wounded commingled.

This a description by a Confederate artillery-man:

"On the slope of a wooded hill our infantry were forming for a charge. Federal infantry were thick in front of them, assisted by artillery, which poured a storm of shrapnel into our ranks. Rhett's battery of our battalion was already blazing away from the crest of the hill, and they were said to have lost thirty men in as many minutes.

" 'Cannoneers, mount! Forward!' "

"Quickly we rushed between the already moving cannon wheels, and nimbly sprang into our seats — all except John Hightower, who missed his hold, and the great heavy weight rolled over his body. Did we halt? No! Not if your brother falls by your side must you heed his dying wail! This is the grim discipline of war.

"Never shall I forget the scene presented on this hill opposite Round Top Mountain. The Federal shrapnel rattled like hail through the trees around us, while our infantry, which was preparing to charge, swayed backward and forward, in and out, a storm cloud vexed by contrary winds."

"Give it to them, boys!" said one of the infantry.

"We'll do it," I responded.

"Ah, I see you are of the right grit."

"When he spoke to me I was repeating the lines —

"For right is right, since God is God,

131

And right the day must win;
To doubt would be disloyalty,
To falter would be sin."

Like many other conceited little beings who inhabit this conceited little world, I presumed to interpret the will of God, and anticipate His policy in the government of this world.

"Fire! Fire! Fire!" And each gun is discharging its leaden terrors into the ranks of the foe. But now comes the brave infantry. Wofford of Georgia, his hat off, and his bald head shining in the sun, dashes through our battery, followed by his brigade. Out flashed Captain Parke's sword, while the words 'Hurrah for you of the bald head' issued from his lips. 'Hurrah for you of the bald head' was repeated by the cannoneers, while the charging Georgians swept down the hillside, driving the retreating foe to the opposite hill."[11]

At this hour I rode up the eastern slope of Little Round Top, tied my horse, clambered over the rocks, and came to the summit, where stood an officer of the Signal Corps and his assistant. The panorama of the battle was before me. At my feet were Plum Rum and a meadow thickly strewn with boulders. Beyond them the Devil's Den, with Ward's brigade and the four guns of Smith's battery upon the crest of the ridge. Northwest of the ledge was Winslow's battery, on the eastern edge of a wheat field; and up the line, beyond another grove, were Bigelow's Ninth Massachusetts, Phillips's Fifth

Massachusetts, and Clark's batteries. In the peach orchard was Hart's; along the Emmitsburg Road a line of guns, all smoking. A white cloud was rising from the woods between the Devil's Den and Rose's house, with rolls of musketry mingling with the cannonade. From the woods by Warfield's house the Confederate cannon were sending solid shot and shells towards the peach orchard. Northward towards the seminary, and the scene of the first day's battle, the Confederate artillery was sending its missiles through the air. Looking towards the cemetery, I saw it covered with a white cloud.

De Trobriand's and Ward's brigades, and Winslow's and Smith's batteries, were confronting Robertson's, Law's, Benning's, Semmes's, Kershaw's, Wofford's, and Anderson's Confederate brigades. Union ambulances were coming out of the woods and moving towards the Taneytown Road. Staff officers were galloping over the fields and pastures, carrying orders. The battle cloud was too dense to see what was going on beyond the Confederate lines, but from the woods came the prolonged yell of the Confederates, mingled with the hurrahs of the Union soldiers. The air was thick with shells. White clouds suddenly burst into view where before there was only the sky. There was a whirring of jagged pieces of iron, mingled with the continuous singing of the leaden rain.

General Meade had authorized Sickles to call upon General Sykes, of the Fifth Corps, for reinforcements, and Barnes's division moved forward towards the wheat field, where Winslow's battery was sending canister into the ranks of the Confederates.

The battle was coming nearer. It began to break at the foot of Little Round Top on the flank of the Fourth Maine. All this time the only persons on Little Round Top were the signal officer and his assistant and myself. Another came, General Warren, engineer in chief of the army. He took a survey of the scene, saw that the Confederates were folding round the left flank of Ward's brigade; that Little Round Top was the key to the position. These his words:

"The whole line of the enemy moved on us in the most confident tones. While I was with the signal officer the musket balls began to fly around us, and he was about to fold up his flags and withdraw, but remained at my request and kept waving them in defiance. Seeing troops going out on the Peach Orchard Road, I rode down the hill, and fortunately met my old brigade, General Ward commanding. It had already passed the point, and I took the responsibility to detach Colonel O'Rorke, the head of whose regiment I had struck, who, on hearing my few words of explanation about the position, moved at once to the hilltop. About this time First Lieutenant Charles E. Hazlett, of the Fifth Artillery, with his battery of rifled cannon, arrived. He comprehended the situation instantly, and planted his guns on the summit of the hill."[12]

Vincent's brigade was also sent by General Sykes on Warren's representations, and came up the hill on the run.

There were too many bullets in the air for the comfort of a noncombatant, and I went down the hill, meeting Vincent's brigade. A few minutes later the battle was raging furiously on the western slope and around the summit.

This the story was told by one of its officers: "Hazlett's battery came rapidly up and plunged directly through our ranks, the horses urged to frantic efforts by the whips of their drivers, and the cannoneers assisting at the wheels. As we reached the crest a never-to-be-forgotten scene burst upon us. A great basin lay before us full of smoke and fire, and literally swarming with riderless horses and fighting, fleeing, and pursuing men. The air was saturated with the sulphurous fumes of battle, and was ringing with the shouts and groans of the combatants. The wild cries of charging lines, the rattle of musketry, the booming of artillery, and the shrieks of the wounded were the orchestral accompaniments of a scene like a very hell itself."[13]

The attack of Hood was upon the position held by Ward's brigade, with the purpose of gaining Little Round Top. The first shock fell upon Ward and De Trobriand; Sweitzer's and Tilton's brigades came to their assistance — Sweitzer in the woods south of the wheat field, and Tilton in the field. Tilton's troops were wholly exposed, while the Confederates were behind a stone wall, and the Union troops were compelled to fall back.

Caldwell's division of the Second Corps came down past Trostle's house. The line formed with Cross's brigade in the woods south of the wheat field, with Brooks's in rear. Kelley's brigade was in the wheat field, and in the grove west of it, with Zook's in the second line. In the struggle Cross and Zook are both mortally wounded.

Like the waves of the sea eddying among the rocks of a rugged shore, so surged the contending forces over the knolls, along the ravines, the roads, and in the wheat field.

Brooks dashed upon Semmes's Confederate brigade and drove it through the woods, across the ravine, past Rose's spring house, to the top of the hill beyond.

The Confederates rallied, and Brooks was driven in turn.

Ayres's division of the Fifth Corps, the regulars of the United States Army, engaged in the conflict, taking the place of Caldwell's division of the Second Corps. In a very short time nearly one-half were killed or wounded. Crawford's division of the Second Corps went down to fight on the same ground. There was much swaying backward and forward in the wheat field, in the woods west and south of it; firing across the stone wall; Confederate brigades striking Union brigades in flank, to find themselves in turn outflanked; the Confederates pushing on with great bravery, persistence, and energy, meeting stubborn resistance, but gradually gaining ground — folding round the left flank of the Union troops — and Robertson's brigade advancing from boulder to boulder, tree to tree, up the southern slope of Little Round Top, till Colonel Chamberlain, commanding the Twentieth Maine, on the left of Vincent's brigade, was obliged to form his troops in the shape of the letter U. The Confederates fire up the hill, picking off the Union officers one by one. Vincent, Weed, Hazlett, all fell, also Colonel O'Rorke.

The Confederates were astonished to receive a volley from behind their backs, coming from a squad of men sheltered behind rocks and trees, fired by the sharpshooters of Stoughton's regiment, whom we saw retreating past Ward's brigade at the beginning of the conflict. Robertson's troops turned to see whence the volley came; Vincent's troops thereupon sprang over the rocks and dashed down the hill, capturing two colonels, fifteen other officers — nearly five hundred prisoners in all — driving the Confederates back to the boulders of the Devil's Den.

We are not to think that there have been silence and inactivity the while by Sherfy's peach orchard and in the fields west of it and southward by Rose's house. From the beginning of the battle the ground has been swept by the Union and Confederate batteries. When Hood's troops came out of the woods by Mr. Warfield's and advanced towards Rose's house, the Union batteries changed their line of fire, making fearful havoc in the ranks of Semmes's brigade. The Fiftieth Georgia lost a third of its men by the enfilading fire of the batteries which Sickles had placed in position east of the orchard.[14]

Kershaw's South Carolinians came through Rose's dooryard with a strong line of skirmishers. At the same moment Barkdale's Mississippians and Wofford's Georgians advanced against the peach orchard. We have seen the whole of the Fifth Corps and two divisions of the Second Corps engaged in the struggle down by the wheat field. Sickles has no reserves; there are no Union troops at hand to help maintain the position at the orchard. Barksdale is grave and impetuous, and urges on his troops.

Sickles sees that he cannot hold the angle. McGilvery orders the batteries in the orchard, also Clark and Phillips, to limber up and hasten to the rear. The regiments of Graham's and Burling's brigades are falling back, fighting obstinately, pressed by Barksdale and the brigades of Anderson from the west, with Kershaw thrusting his troops into the gap east of the orchard. They must fall back or be cut off. The batteries from the orchard, leaving many of their horses killed or wounded behind them, make their way eastward past Trostle's house, the men tugging at the wheels to help the limping, wounded animals.

McGilvery rides to Captain Bigelow, commanding the Ninth Massachusetts. "Limber up and get out as quick as you can," he shouts.

"I shall lose all my men in limbering up, but I can retire by prolong;" and the gunners stretch out the ropes, hitch the horses to them, and so, loading his cannon with double charges of canister, he begins to fall back through the field towards Trostle's house, firing at Kershaw advancing through the field south of the road. But down through the peach orchard came Barksdale, following the retreating troops of Burling and Graham.

"Keep back Kershaw's skirmishers with canister," was Bigelow's order to Lieutenant Milton, commanding two guns on the left. "Send solid shot into Barksdale's men," the order to Lieutenants Erickson and Whitaker.[15]

To keep clear of the fire of the cannon a portion of Barksdale's troops moved to the right. The guns were in Trostle's dooryard, and a portion of the Mississippians ran to gain the shelter of the barn, firing from the windows. The Twenty-first Mississippi advanced directly down the road and across the field from the orchard. Kershaw meanwhile was advancing on the left, the South Carolinians jumping over a wall and creeping, under its shelter, towards the battery.

No infantry supports, except a handful of men — not a dozen in all — of the One Hundred and Eighteenth Pennsylvania, of Tilton's brigade, are at hand. Graham's and Brewster's brigades have been pushed back; Humphreys's division is changing front to meet Barksdale, widening the gap by Trostle's.

It is the crisis of the conflict, the moment of the struggle on Little Round Top. McGilvery, leaving the Ninth Massachusetts Battery to hold to the last position at Trostle's, is bringing twenty-five guns into position along the ridge. These were his parting words to Bigelow:

"There is not an infantryman back of you; you must remain and sacrifice your battery if need be until I can find some batteries to put in position and cover you."[16]

Down upon the battery came the Mississippians, shooting horses and men, receiving double-shotted charges till the canister was all gone. Lieutenant Milton, seeing the horses of the other pieces dropping, tore down a gap in the wall, leaped his over it, and escaped with two pieces; but those attached to the other guns were shot.

Some of the men were killed, but the living bore the rammers and sponges from the field so that the Confederates could not use the guns. Captain Bigelow is wounded, and falls from his horse. Lieutenant Erickson, twice wounded, falls beside his gun, and his horse goes upon the run into the lines of the Mississippians. Lieutenant Whitaker is wounded, but escapes. Bigelow is lifted upon another horse and reaches the rear. One cannoneer is killed while trying to spike his gun. Of the four battery officers one is killed, another mortally wounded, the third slightly wounded. Of seven sergeants two are killed and four wounded. Eighty out of the eighty-eight horses have been shot. The battery has been sacrificed, but it has accomplished a great end in delaying for half an hour the advance of Kershaw and Barksdale, who otherwise would have had a clear and unopposed passage to the crest of the ridge.

General Sickles was wounded by Trostle's barn, and Hancock, of the Second Corps, was sent by General Meade to take command.

The Mississippians gave a shout of victory when they seized Bigelow's four guns. In the rush their lines had been broken, and it took time for them to reform. South of them Wofford was pushing towards the ridge, when there came a sheet of flame from its crest. It was McGilvery's opening fire — so destructive that the Georgians could not face it, but were compelled to find shelter behind rocks, trees, and fences.

We have seen Caldwell's and Ayres's divisions of the Second Corps engaged in the struggle in front of Little Round Top. Hancock has only Gibbon's division remaining. It is seven o'clock; the sun a half hour above the horizon. Humphreys's division of the Third Corps is still holding the Emmitsburg Road by Codori's, but its left flank, instead of facing west, is formed to face south to meet Barksdale.

The time has come for Longstreet to hurl the whole of Anderson's division of Confederates into the conflict; and Wilcox's brigade comes across the road a little south of the house where

Josephine Miller baked her bread, falling upon the Union batteries before the drivers could hitch on the horses.

"We rushed forward and captured several pieces of artillery and caissons. Some of them were defended very gallantly, firing grape at us when within fifty yards or less. One little fellow, apparently not more than fourteen, sat erect on the lead horse, looking straight at the front, trying to whip his horses forward. His two wheelhorses had been shot, and he did not know it. While I was admiring him some excited Confederates, to my inexpressible regret, shot him down. We halted and sheltered ourselves as best we could, and kept up the fight for perhaps half an hour. One time, evidently without loaded guns, the enemy charged up very close — say within forty yards — but were driven. At last our line was broken on the left, and we fell back, but could not take the captured cannon."[17]

In the meadow east of Codori's house the battle rages with great fury. Hancock sees that it is a critical moment, and sends General Willard with three regiments to meet Barksdale, who is riding everywhere, urging on his men — a conspicuous figure. It is his nature to be aggressive. His speeches in Congress, before the war, were ever vehement. He has pressed the conflict; has captured four guns. A little farther and he will be upon Cemetery Ridge. Suddenly he reels in his saddle. A bullet has pierced him, and he falls with a mortal wound. Willard's men rush past him, driving the Mississippians, who in turn rally to rescue their wounded leader. Willard also falls with a mortal wound.

We are not to think that the men of the Third Corps, who have been forced back from the road and the orchard, have fled; on the contrary, though the ranks are broken and in disorder, the ground is held with great obstinacy. Hancock has ordered in nearly all of Gibbon's division. General Meade has ordered Slocum from Culp's Hill, and the troops of the Sixth and Twelfth Corps are coming, but will they be in season to roll back the Confederates before they gain possession of the ridge? The sun is sinking; men can see but dimly through the murky battle clouds. Hancock discovers Wilcox's Confederate brigade, thinks the troops a part of his own command, rides towards them, but is welcomed by a volley which brings down his aide, Captain Miller.[18] Upon the ridge behind him is Thomas's battery, with eight companies of the First Minnesota Regiment (Colonel Coville) supporting it — two hundred and fifty-two men. Hancock rides up to the regiment. This the story as told by one of its officers:

"Just then Hancock rode up, and, unable to conceal his agitation, asked, in almost anguished tones, 'Great God, is this all the men we have here?' . . . Not a hundred yards behind us was the Taneytown Road, crowded with our wagons, and beyond them the hospitals and trains. If Hancock could only stop that charging mass for five minutes. Pointing to the smoke-covered masses of the advancing foe, he cried, 'Colonel Coville, advance and take those colors!' "

" 'Forward!' " shouted our gallant colonel; and as one man the regiment arose, and, as if on review, stepped down the slope towards the enemy. Their cannon opened on us, and shell and solid shot tore through the ranks, and the more deadly Enfield rifles of their infantry were centred on us alone. At every step fall our men, but no one wavers. Every gap is closed up, and, bringing down their bayonets, the boys press shoulder to shoulder. Five color bearers are shot down, and five times our flag goes proudly forward. Within a hundred — within fifty yards of the fire, one-quarter of our men already fallen and yet no shot has been fired.

"Charge!" rang the order along the line, and with a wild cheer we ran at them.

"Their extended line swept round our flanks like the waters around a rock; but before us they gave way, for we empty our guns with the muzzles at their very hearts. A perfect swath of men sink upon the ground, and their living recoil back upon their second line. Their supporting lines, confused and excited, wildly commence firing through the mass in front, slaughtering their own men and throwing them into confusion.

"Our object had been obtained. At the instant, a battery on our left opened and poured a few rapid volleys into the confused mass, and swept it from the field. The enemy had disappeared, all but their dead and wounded, and over their prostrate bodies rang the hearty cheers of our reinforcing troops. The almost fatal attack of the Confederates had been repulsed, but where was the First Minnesota? Only forty-seven men now gathered around our colors — two hundred and five killed and wounded — none missing. It was the Thermopylae of our regiment."[19]

It was the twenty-five guns of McGilvery, together with Thomas's battery, which hurled canister into the ranks of the Confederates.

The critical moment had come and gone, for in the gloaming the troops of the Sixth and Twelfth Corps, and Stannard's Vermont Brigade, attached to the First Corps, were forming on Cemetery Ridge, and it was their cheers which rang through the enveloping battle cloud.

Longstreet examined the Union lines. He saw that it would be a useless sacrifice to attempt to force them, and so the sound of the strife died away, the cannons' lips were cooling, and the wearied soldiers of both armies threw themselves upon the ground for rest; the Confederates in the fields along the Emmitsburg Road, and behind the ledges of the Devil's Den, and in the fields between Rose's house and the orchard.

Though the contest had ceased in the fields around Codori's and Trostle's farmhouses, it began suddenly amid the woods on Culp's Hill and on the northern slope of Cemetery Hill.

Johnson's division of Ewell's corps was

advancing to turn the right flank of the Union army. All of the Twelfth Corps, with the exception of Green's brigade, had been taken from Culp's Hill to roll back the Confederates under Longstreet. Green had drawn out his brigade into a thin line to hold all the ground. The Union troops had thrown up breastworks, but Johnson captured them with ease, and, satisfied with what he had done — not knowing that thirty rods farther, and he would be in possession of the Baltimore Turnpike — rested for the night.

It was nine o'clock when Hays's and Hoke's brigades of Early's division, creeping stealthily along a hedge fence at the foot of the northern slope of Cemetery Hill, with a yell, rushed upon Weiderick's battery and Ames's brigade of the Eleventh Corps. There was a fierce struggle, hand-to-hand fights, the cannoneers wielding their rammers. One Union soldier seized a stone and hurled it upon a Confederate, dashing out his brains. Sergeant Geible, of the One Hundred and Seventh Ohio, carrying the colors, was shot. A Confederate soldier seized them. Adjutant Young shot him with his revolver, but the next moment two bullets pierced him. A Confederate officer aimed a blow at his head, which Lieutenant Suhrer parried, and the colors were saved.

The Union troops in the field north of the turnpike were driven, and Confederates for a few moments held the cannon, but the Fifth Maine Battery, under Lieutenant Whittier, on the western slope of Culp's Hill, opened upon the Confederates with an enfilading fire. Eustis's brigade, behind a wall in the hollow east of the hill, fired to the left oblique. Carroll's brigade came upon the double-quick across the eastern slope of Cemetery Hill, sent by Hancock, and the Confederates were driven, leaving the ground thickly strewn with killed and wounded.

It was ten o'clock before the contest ended. So closed the second day.

# Chapter 5

## *Cemetery Ridge*

*What next* shall be done? This the great question ever confronting a general commanding an army. In battle he must be quick to decide. General Lee did not hesitate. He called no council of his officers, but acted on his own judgment. Stuart had arrived at last with the cavalry, after a long ride from Carlisle. A. P. Hill and Ewell had swept the First and Eleventh Union Corps from their position on the first day. Longstreet had pushed the Third Corps from the Emmitsburg Road, had all but gained Little Round Top, had compelled Meade to hurry a portion of the Twelfth Corps from Culp's Hill, which enabled Johnson's division of Ewell's corps to gain possession of a coveted position without fighting a battle. Johnson was where he could threaten Meade's right and rear, only a short distance from the Baltimore Turnpike. Stuart had come down from the north, and was in the best possible position to act in concert with Johnson, and make havoc of Meade's trains. Pickett's division of Longstreet's corps had arrived from Cashtown. Johnson's and Pickett's troops were fresh, and so were Posey's and Mahone's brigades of Hill's corps, and Smith's, of Ewell's. Longstreet's success in pushing the Third Corps from the Emmitsburg Road would enable him to plant all the artillery along that position, and pour a destructive fire upon the centre of Meade's line; and at the right moment he would hurl Pickett and Anderson upon that point, break through, and, in conjunction with Johnson's division on Culp's Hill and Stuart with the cavalry, make the rout of the Union army complete. That the plan of General Lee, who ordered Ewell to begin the attack at daylight. Johnson was reinforced by Daniel's and O'Neal's brigades.

Early in the morning General Lee rode to Longstreet's headquarters. "General," said Longstreet, "I have had my scouts out all night, and I find that you still have an excellent opportunity to move around to the right of Meade's army and maneuvers him into attacking us."[1]

"The enemy is there, and I am going to strike him," Lee replied, pointing towards Cemetery Hill.

"General, I have been a soldier all my life. I have been with soldiers engaged in fights by couples, by squads, companies, regiments, divisions, and armies, and should know as well as any one what soldiers can do. It is my opinion that no fifteen thousand men ever arrayed for battle can take that position."

General Lee entered upon no argument, but

directed Longstreet to prepare Pickett's division for the attack. These were Longstreet's words: "I should not have been so urgent had I not foreseen the hopelessness of the proposed assault. I felt that I must say a word against the sacrifice of my men; I felt that my motives were such that General Lee would or could not misconstrue them. I said no more, however, but turned away."

General Meade had been turning over the great question as to what should be done. Ought not the army to fall back to a stronger position, where, joined by reinforcements, it could make victory sure? In the first day's battle the First and Eleventh Corps were cut to pieces. Thousands of stragglers had made their way towards Westminster and Taneytown. In the fight of the second day the Third Corps, small at the beginning, had suffered fearful loss. The Fifth Corps had made frightful sacrifices; the Second Corps had lost many men; the Sixth and Twelfth Corps alone were fresh. General Meade held a consultation of his corps commanders. The majority were opposed to retreating. To retreat would be acknowledgment of defeat; the army was not defeated. If it had suffered great losses Lee's had been greater, so they reasoned.

I passed the night in a small house near Rock Creek, a short distance south of the turnpike. I did not know that I was within musket shot of the extreme left of the Confederate line, with only the pickets between. I was early in the saddle, and found Ruger's division of the Twelfth Corps was lying in the pastures along the Baltimore Turnpike. On the two hills south were three batteries of the Reserve Artillery, the cannon pointing north, to rain shells upon the woods where the Confederates were holding the Union breastworks, which they had seized in the night.

The clouds hung low upon the hills. It was a sultry morning. I heard two guns, deep and heavy, breaking the stillness; two more, and then the uproar began. They were Union cannon. General Meade had taken the offensive, determined to recover Culp's Hill. It was an announcement to General Lee that the Union army was to fight it out upon the spot; that, instead of being disheartened, it was about to put forth its aggressive strength.

Emerging from a grove, the scene burst upon me. The cemetery, Powers's Hill, and McAllister's Hill, south of the turnpike, were aflame, sending shells into the green wood north of the turnpike. There were a few musket shots from the skirmishers in the woods upon the hill. Slocum's troops were preparing for the assault.

The four brigades which left Culp's Hill and went upon the double-quick towards Little Round Top at sunset returned to the Baltimore Turnpike at eleven in the night, to find that the Confederates had quietly taken possession of the breastworks which they had constructed. There was a grim humor about it which the men of the

Twelfth Corps did not relish, and which put them on their mettle.

Green's brigade of Gear's division was holding the western slope of the hill; Kane's and Candy's brigades stood next in line; Ruger's division occupied the ground east to Rock Creek; Lockwood's brigade faced north, McDougall's northwest, Colgrove's west.

East of the creek Neill's brigade of the Sixth Corps held the left of the line. In the rear of Geary were Shaler's and Wheaton's brigades of the Sixth Corps.

General Ewell had no artillery in position to reply to the Union guns, and his troops, sheltered by the thick forest and the breastworks, suffered little from the cannonade. But an artillery fire long sustained is trying to the best-trained troops, though they have marched to victory under a leader like Stonewall Jackson.

Colonel Colgrove's brigade formed in a grove between the turnpike and Rock Creek, the Twenty-seventh Indiana on the right; then the Second Massachusetts. They were to charge across the marshy lowland and the brook which winds through it, to strike the left of the Confederate line. It was but a few rods; five minutes would suffice to carry them across the meadow. The signal was given, and they moved on. There came a volley. Men dropped, but the living went forward upon the run.

Five minutes, and the remnant drifted back — broken, shattered.

On a granite boulder near the eastern edge of the meadow stands a tablet erected by the survivors of the Second Massachusetts. Thus it reads: "From the hill behind this monument, on the morning of July 3, 1863, the Second Massachusetts Infantry made an assault upon the Confederate troops in the works at the base of Culp's Hill, opposite. The regiment carried into the charge twenty-two officers and two hundred and ninety-four enlisted men. It lost four officers and forty-one enlisted men killed, and six officers and eighty-four enlisted men wounded."

Back over the meadow they retreated, followed by the exultant Confederates; but they reformed amid the trees, faced about, and strewed the ground with Confederate dead by their deliberate volleys.

Johnson was just ready to advance when Slocum began the assault. Had the Union army waited a few minutes, the struggle would have been along the Baltimore Pike, instead of in the woods and along the boulders on Culp's Hill. Johnson could not, from the nature of the ground, bring forward his artillery, and after the first cannonade by the Union batteries the battle was wholly by the infantry.

From seven o'clock till eleven there was a ceaseless tempest, wholly in the woods, for the possession of the breastworks, men firing from behind trees and boulders. The oaks were pitted with bullets. Gradually the Confederates were pushed back, losing at last, in a charge by the

Union troops, three stands of colors and five hundred prisoners, besides more than two thousand killed and wounded. At eleven o'clock the Union line was intact once more, holding the ground from Culp's Hill to Cemetery Hill, and thence to the summit of Great Round Top, with breastworks nearly the entire distance. Through the night and morning the soldiers had been at work with shovels and axes, and the line was stronger than ever.

Lee has one division (Pickett's, of Longstreet's corps) which had taken no part in the battle. The troops had arrived from Chambersburg. They were eager to take part in the struggle. Anderson's division of Hill's corps was comparatively fresh, having taken but little part since the afternoon of the first day. With such a body, numbering about fifteen thousand men, he would strike the last great blow.

The Union signal officer on Round Top, looking westward over fields and groves, could see the Confederate troops gathering in the woods south of the seminary. He caught glimpses of batteries coming into position.

The cemetery ridge south of Zeigler's Grove is lower than the ground by Codori's house. General Lee confidently believed that he could open fire with all his artillery upon the Union lines from an assaulting column in the woods west of Codori's house; that when the Union line had been demoralized by the cannonade he could sweep the troops across the field west of the

Emmitsburg Road, hurl them like a thunderbolt upon the Union troops south of Zeigler's Grove, divide Meade's line at the centre, folding the two halves back — one upon Little Round Top, the other upon Culp's Hill — as he would open two folding doors, thus winning the victory — a single crushing blow. At the same moment he would have Stuart with the cavalry gain the rear of the Union army, east of Culp's Hill, fall upon Meade's wagons, and make the rout complete.

I was at Meade's headquarters when an officer came from Cemetery Hill with a message from General Howard that the Confederate cavalry could be seen moving eastward. The divisions of Union cavalry, Gregg's and Kilpatrick's, were by Rock Creek, near the Baltimore Turnpike, watering their horses. It was past eleven o'clock when a messenger rode down with an order for Gregg to go out and meet Stuart, and for Kilpatrick to go south of Round Top and fall upon the extreme right of Longstreet.

"Bugler, blow your horn! Come on, boys!" said Kilpatrick. The clear notes of the cornet rang out, and Kilpatrick's division turned south. I joined General Gregg's division, which went upon a trot down the turnpike a short distance, then northeast through the fields and pastures. We soon came in sight of the Confederate cavalry.

Gregg had three regiments of McIntosh's brigade, Costar's and Irvin Gregg's brigades, Randol's and Pennington's batteries — almost

155

five thousand men.

Stuart had Thompson's, W. H. F. Lee's, Fitzhugh Lee's, and Jenkins's brigades — nearly seven thousand.

A road runs north from the Baltimore Pike, and crosses the Bonnaughtown Road, and is known as the Low Dutch, or Salem Church Road. The house of Mr. Reeves stands at the crossing.

A portion of the Confederates had come down into the field, but after a few cannon shot they fell back. Thinking that there might not be an immediate engagement, I rode to a large farmhouse, where I found a woman and her four daughters hard at work baking bread for the soldiers. I was at the dinner table when one of the daughters came in, exclaiming that the Confederates were coming. Stepping to the door, I saw a regiment wheeling into line in the field but a short distance from the monument which now marks the scene of the conflict. My horse was eating his oats in the dooryard, and I had not finished my own dinner. The Confederates might be sweeping down upon the house, but I was a citizen, and they probably would not molest me. Besides, the Union cavalry were forming to confront them, so, standing upon the flank of both Union and Confederate, I saw the rush — the gleaming of sabres, the carbines' flashes, pistol shots, horses leaping and plunging, riders going down, and the retreat of the Confederates to the field north of Mr. Rummel's house. For a time there was inaction; Gregg was standing on the defensive. He was to keep Stuart from gaining the Baltimore Turnpike.

Thinking that there might not be any serious engagement, I left the cavalry and rode towards the cemetery once more, for a cannonade was going on, mingled with a rippling of musketry. West of the Emmitsburg Road, between Codori's house and the seminary, stood the farmhouse of Mr. Bliss, who had a large barn, the lower story of which was of brick. The Confederate skirmishers had used it on the morning of the second, but had been driven out by the Twelfth New Jersey; but they were again in the barn, firing from the windows, picking off the Union troops. The batteries in the cemetery sent shells and solid shot into the building, but the Confederates crouched beneath the brick walls and still remained. The Fourteenth Connecticut, of Smyth's brigade, was detailed to drive them out. Eight companies went down through the field. Men began to drop. "Scatter and run!" was the order shouted by General Hays, commanding the division. The ranks divided and rushed on, and drove out the Confederates; but they rallied in the orchard, and others came to assist them. It was an engagement to see which should have possession of the premises. General Hays determined to settle the matter. The Confederates saw an officer riding down from the Union line. The sharpshooters aimed at him, bullets sang about his ears, but he kept straight on.

"General Hays orders that you set the buildings on fire," he shouted to the officer commanding the Connecticut men, then turned and rode back, the bullets spinning past him. He reached the crest of the ridge, raised his hat and saluted the Confederates, who, admiring his coolness and bravery, sent out a heart cheer. It was Captain Postles, of the First Delaware. A moment later the flames were rising from the house and barn, and adding another feature to the lurid scene.

Indications pointed to a renewal of battle on the past of the Confederates, and every Union officer was on the alert — especially along the ridge between Zeigler's Grove and Little Round Top, the point where the attack was likely to be made. Robinson's division of the First Corps was in the grove. Then came Hays's division of the Second Corps, the front line along a low stone wall, the second line east of the crest of the ridge. Beyond Hays's division was Gibbon's, behind a rail fence. The soldiers had taken down the rails, laid them in a pile, and through the forenoon had scooped a shallow trench, in which they were lying. A small copse of scrubby oaks marked the position. Three regiments of Stannard's Vermont Brigade were in front of the main line, around a copse of trees and tangled vines.

The troops selected by General Lee to make the attack, or to cooperate in it, were Hill's corps and Pickett's division of Longstreet's — in all, twenty-one brigades, under the direction of Longstreet, that there might be united action under one commander. Pickett's, Anderson's, and Heth's divisions were to lead in the assault, to be supported by Pender's, Trimble's, and Rodes's divisions. To insure success the troops were to advance in a column or lines of brigades. On the right of the line in front was Kemper's brigade, with Armistead in the second line; then Garnet and Scales, Archer and Field, Lane and Pettigrew; to be followed on the right by Wilcox and Perry, in the centre by Wright, on the left by Posey and McGowan, Thomas's and Rodes's divisions of Ewell's corps.

General Armistead was riding along his brigade, and came to the Fifty-third Virginia, and called out Robert Tyler, the seventeen-year-old grandson of President Tyler, who carried the colors.

"Do you see those breastworks over yonder?" he asked.

"Yes, sir."

"Well, I want you to plant that flag on them."

"General, I will do it or die," said the boy.[2]

Colonel Alexander through the morning had been arranging the Confederate artillery. He had seventy-five cannon at the peach orchard and vicinity, and along the woods behind Hill's troops sixty-three more — one hundred and thirty-eight — which were to fire directly upon the cemetery and the ridge south of it.[3] When the infantry brigades were all in position ready to advance, General Longstreet was to fire two cannon as the signal for the opening of the cannonade, which it was supposed would silence the Union artillery, and so demoralize the Union troops that Pickett and Anderson would sweep all before them.

General Hunt, commanding the Union artillery, was arranging his batteries. This his account:

"Compactly arranged on the crest of the ridge was McGilvery's artillery — forty-one guns. Well to the right, in front of Hays and Gibbon, was the artillery of the Second Corps, under its chief, Captain Hazard. Woodruff's battery was in Zeigler's Grove; on his left, in succession, Arnold's Rhode Island, Cushing's United States, Brown's Rhode Island, and Rorty's New York; total number in the corps, twenty-six. Daniel's battery of horse artillery, four guns, was between McGilvery and Hazard. In addition, some of the guns on Cemetery Hill, and Rittenhouse's battery, on Little Round Top, could be brought to bear; but these were offset by batteries similarly placed on the flanks of the enemy, so that in the Second Corps line, within the space of a mile, were seventy-one guns to oppose nearly one hundred and fifty. They were on an open crest, plainly visible from all parts of the line." . . .[4]

This the scene at eleven o'clock:

"Our whole front for two miles was covered by (Confederate) batteries already in line or going

160

into position. They stretched, apparently in one unbroken mass, from opposite the town to the peach orchard, which bounded the view to the left, the ridges of which were planted thick with cannon. Never before had such a sight been witnessed on this continent, and rarely, if ever, abroad. What did it mean? It might possibly be to hold that line while its infantry was sent to aid Ewell, or to guard against a counterstroke from us; but it most probably meant an assault on our centre, to be preceded by a cannonade in order to crush our batteries and shake our infantry — at least to cause us to exhaust our ammunition in reply, so that the assaulting troops might pass in good condition over the half mile of open ground which was beyond our effective musketry fire."

General Hunt believed that it was to be a direct assault by a body of troops concealed in the woods south of the seminary, and made arrangements to meet it. These were his instructions:

"Beginning at the right, I instructed the chiefs of artillery and battery commanders to withhold their fire for fifteen or twenty minutes after the cannonade commenced, then to concentrate their fire, with all possible accuracy, on those batteries which were most destructive to us, but slowly, so that when the enemy's ammunition was exhausted, we should have sufficient left to meet the assault."

Neither General Hunt nor General Meade

issued any orders to the Union artillery to prevent the Confederate artillery from coming into position. "The enemy, conscious of the strength of his position, simply sat still and waited for us," writes Colonel Alexander, of the Confederate artillery.

General Longstreet did not approve of the contemplated attack, and was greatly depressed in spirits.[5] His troops were to make what he believed to be a hopeless charge; that they would be sacrificed with nothing gained, and that he would be obliged to issue the order. He could not do it, and at noon sent this note to Colonel Alexander:

"Colonel, — If the artillery fire does not have the effect to drive off the enemy or greatly demoralize him, so as to make our efforts pretty certain, I would prefer that you should not advise General Pickett to make the charge. I shall rely greatly on your good judgment to determine the matter, and shall expect you to let General Pickett know when the moment offers."

It was a startling note, and Colonel Alexander, who shrank from taking such a responsibility, sent this reply:

"I will not be able to judge of the effect of our fire on the enemy except by his return fire, for his infantry is but little exposed to view, and the smoke will obscure the whole field. If, as I infer from your note, there is any alternative to this attack, it should be carefully considered before opening our fire, for it will take all the artillery ammunition we have left to test this one thoroughly, and if the result is unfavorable we will have none left for another effort. And even if this is entirely successful, it can only be so at a very bloody cost."

Colonel Alexander a few moments later received a reply from Longstreet:

"The intention is to advance the infantry if the artillery has the desired effect of driving the enemy's off, or having other effect such as to warrant us in making the attack. When the moment arrives, advise General Pickett, and of course advance such artillery as you can use in aiding the attack."

General Wright, who was in the attack on the evening of the second, was with Colonel Alexander, and read the notes.

"It is not so hard to *go there* as it looks; I was nearly there with my brigade yesterday. The trouble is to stay there. The whole Yankee army is there in a bunch."[6]

Colonel Alexander rode to General Pickett, and found that he was sanguine as to the result. He and his troops were in the best of spirits. They had been resting after their march of the morning. They had heard of the success of Hill's and Ewell's troops on the first day, and how Longstreet and McLaws had driven the Union troops from the peach orchard and the Emmitsburg Road, and it was left for them, with the aid of Hill's troops, to complete the victory, and win the great decisive battle which would give the Confederacy a place among the nations. Not a man doubted it. General Pickett was so certain as to what the result would be that Colonel Alexander determined there should be no indecision on his part. This the note which he sent to Longstreet: "When our artillery fire is at its best, I shall order Pickett to charge."

I had nearly reached Meade's headquarters from the position occupied by the cavalry, when I heard two cannon — the guns agreed upon as the signal on the part of the Confederate artillery. My watch, set to Washington time, pointed to five minutes past one.

The guns were fired by Lieutenant Brown's section of the First Company of Washington Artillery.[7] Instantly from below the peach orchard, northward to the Theological Seminary, from Benner's Hill, northeast of Gettysburg, not only from the one hundred and thirty-eight cannon which Alexander had arranged, but from Ewell's guns, more than one hundred and fifty in all, came solid shot and shells. The air seemed to be full of missiles. A moment later there came a crash from the Union artillery — all the batteries — those on Little Round Top, along the ridge, in the cemetery, round to the western slope of Culp's Hill. The instructions of General Hunt were for the batteries to wait a little while before replying, but flesh and blood could not wait. Nor can I see that anything would have been gained by waiting. The Confederate fire from the outset was destructive, and equally damaging was that of the Union cannon. This the record of Colonel Alexander:

"In a minute every gun was at work. The enemy were not slow in coming back on us, and the grand roar of nearly the whole artillery of both armies burst in on the silence almost as suddenly as the full notes of an organ could fill a church. . . . The enemy's position seemed to have broken out with guns everywhere, and from Round Top to Cemetery Hill was blazing like a volcano. The air seemed full of missiles from every direction."

A Confederate shell exploding in the cemetery killed or wounded twenty-seven men. General Meade's headquarters were directly in the line of fire from the one hundred and thirty-eight Confederate cannon. Solid shot tore through the house. Shells exploded in the dooryard, wounding horses, cutting down the peach trees, ripping open bags of oats, sending General Meade, his staff, and the newspaper correspondents for shelter elsewhere — General Meade into the woods eastward, where his headquarters flag was stuck in the ground beside a huge boulder. Not that General Meade attempted to screen himself or staff, but to prudently find a place less exposed than the cottage of Mrs. Leister, whose roof could be plainly seen by the Confederates at the peach orchard. One hundred missiles a minute swept across the ridge, crashing through baggage wagons, ambulances, exploding caissons, and adding confusion and horror to the scene.

A soldier lying on the ground not far from me is suddenly whirled into the air. I hear the whir of the approaching shell; the next moment the living form is a mass of mangled flesh, broken bones, and streaming blood.

For nearly an hour the terrible storm howls and rages, and then there comes a sudden silence on the part of the Union guns.

General Hunt, comprehending the intention of Lee that the cannonade was to be followed by an advance, wishing to have a supply of ammunition at the decisive moment, directed the batteries to cease firing. The gunners throw themselves upon the ground beside their pieces.

General Longstreet was with General Pickett. A courier came with a note from Colonel Alexander to Pickett, written five minutes before the Union artillery ceased:

"If you are coming at all you must come at once, or I cannot give you proper support; but the enemy's fire has not slackened at all — at least eighteen guns are still firing from the cemetery itself,"[8] read the note. Five minutes passed, and the brazen lips of all the Union cannon were silent, and the guns in the cemetery limbered up and disappeared. The Confederate artillery has not ceased, but the cannon are firing with greater vigor, now that no answering shot comes from the cemetery ridge.

"If he does not run up fresh batteries in five

minutes this is our fight," says Colonel Alexander, who is looking through his glass towards the cemetery, where he can see the ground thickly strewn with dead horses and men. The five minutes pass; no batteries come to take the place of those which had disappeared.

Colonel Alexander does not know that Major Osborne, commanding the Union guns in the cemetery, is only biding his time; that his batteries are resting behind the cemetery; that in a twinkling they will be flaming again. He does not mistrust that General Hunt has anticipated just what the Confederate movement is to be; that the tempest will be more terrific than ever when the time comes for action.

Colonel Alexander shuts his glass, and writes once more:

"For God's sake come quick. The eighteen minutes are gone; come quick, or my ammunition won't let me support you properly."

The messenger hands it to Pickett, who reads it and passes it to Longstreet.

"Shall I advance?"[9]

No word in reply; only a bow from Longstreet, as he mounts his horse.

"I shall lead my division forward, sir."

Longstreet makes no reply, but rides away.

This was the scene of the moment as given by a Confederate:

"While Longstreet was still speaking, Pickett's division swept out of the woods, and showed the full length of its gray ranks and shining bayonets, as grand a sight as every man looked on. Joining it on the left, Pettigrew stretched farther than I could see. Gen. Dick Garnett, just out of a sick ambulance, and buttoned up in an old blue over-coat, riding at the head of his brigade, passed us and saluted Longstreet."[10]

At the moment, I was near the cemetery and heard a chorus of voices saying, "There they come!" Up from the ground sprang the cannon-eers, who ran their guns forward into position and began to fire. At the same moment the cannon of Little Round Top broke the silence. The Union cannon along the ridge were still dumb. Their time had not come. The Confed-erate cannon ceased, to enable the infantry to advance, but after the troops had moved on, renewed their fire.

Up in the cemetery, General Howard, watching the advancing Confederates, turned to Major Osborne, commanding the artillery, and said, "The Second Corps and the artillery will take care of the assaulting column; concentrate your fire upon their supports;"[11] and the ceme-tery cannon opened a destructive enfilading fire upon the troops which General Lee intended should drive home the wedge which Pickett, Anderson, and Heth were to insert in the Union line.

The front line of the Confederates reaches the Emmitsburg Road, the Union pickets falling back, to be out of the line of fire which they know will soon open. There is an ominous silence along Cemetery Ridge. Says Hancock in his account: "The column pressed on, coming within musketry range, our men evincing a striking disposition to withhold their fire until it could be delivered with deadly effect."

The Confederates are crossing the road north of Codori's house, when the cannon on the ridge open upon them. They descend the gentle slope, and then comes the first roll of musketry from the two Vermont regiments thrown out in front of the main line, sending an oblique fire upon Kemper, who moves on to strike the Second Corps. The Confederates are between the road and the low stone wall behind which Gibbon's and Hays's troops are lying, when the first hot blast from the front bursts upon them. They come to a halt and return the fire — loading, firing, again advancing. Garnett falls dead; Kemper goes down wounded; Armistead, gray haired — the only general officer of the division after Pickett — waves his sword. "Come on, boys!" he shouts, and they rush on towards the wall — he to fall mortally wounded.[12]

The supporting brigades on the left at this moment were coming within canister range, and the double-shotted cannon in the cemetery were cutting them to pieces, the howitzers firing twice in sixty seconds — a death-tempest so pitiless that the brigades melted away as the snowflake in the running stream, the regiments breaking and disappearing. Officers tried to rally them, but in vain. "Pickett galloped down and implored them to rally, but they were panic stricken, and no effort could induce them to form anew while under that terrific storm of fire," writes a Confederate officer.[13]

## Note to Second Day's Engagement

1. Sherfy's house and peach orchard.
2. Position of Fifth and Ninth Massachusetts batteries.
3. Trostle's house.
4. Wheat field, and right of Ward's brigade.
5. Peter Rogers's house.
6. Codori's house and barn. Humphreys's division extended from this point along the Emmitsburg Road, past Rogers's house.
7. Cemetery Hill.
8. Where McGilvery massed his guns. The line selected by General Sickles extended from Codori's south to Sherfy's orchard, figure 1; then to figure 2, where it crossed the road. Burling's brigade in part occupied the wood to the left of figure 2; Winslow's battery was at figure 4; Ward's brigade extended through the woods to the left, to the Devil's Den, not seen in the view. On the Union side, Birney's division of the Third Corps, the Fifth Corps, and Caldwell's division of the Second Corps, fought to the left of figures 2–4.

On the Confederate side were Hood's and McLaws's divisions of Longstreet's corps.

Hood's movement was to gain Little Round Top. The retreat of the Union troops was across the ground between Little Round Top and Trostle's house, back to figure 8. Kershaw's Confederate brigade advanced through the woods to the left of figure 3; Barksdale advanced between figures 3 and 5; Wilcox's and the other brigades of Hill's corps, under figure 6.

Willard's brigade of the Second Corps and the First Minnesota Regiment advanced from the position between figures 7 and 8, drove the Confederates to figure 6, and recaptured the Union cannon left in the retreat.

### Note to Third Day's Engagement

The Union line extended from Little Round Top to figure 7. Stannard's brigade was in advance of the main line, at figure 9; the advance of Pickett and Anderson was from figures 1, 3, 5, and 6, across the open field between figures 5 and 6; Pickett crossed the road between figures 6 and 7; Wilcox, who was in the rear of Pickett, crossed the road between figures 5 and 6. The third Confederate line was in the open field between figures 5 and 6, and was cut to pieces by the cannon on Little Round Top and those on Cemetery Hill, figure 7.

When Pickett reached the stone wall between figures 7 and 8, Stannard's brigade at figure 9 made its flank movement northward towards figure 7, the farthest point reached by the Confederates. Figure 10 is Culp's Hill, the extreme left of the Union line.

The brigades of Pickett are up to the stone wall, pouring their volleys into the faces of the Sixty-ninth and Seventy-first Pennsylvania of Webb's brigade, which are pushed back by Armistead's men, Robert Tyler, true to his promise, planting his colors on the wall. All of the guards are killed; the colors are shot to pieces. A bullet tears through Tyler's shoulder, and he and the flag go down together. He tries to rise, but a second bullet inflicts a mortal wound.[14]

The Confederates rush up to the muzzles of Cushing's cannon. Cushing fires his last shot and falls dead beside his guns. There is a desperate struggle — the bayonet thrust, pistol shot, clubbing of muskets, men summoning all their strength into a supreme effort. Hancock is everywhere along the line. [15] "Strike them in flank!" he shouts to Stannard; and the Vermonters make a half-wheel to the right, march north, and deliver their volleys.

"Where shall we go in?" Colonel Devereux, of the Nineteenth Massachusetts, of Hall's brigade, in the second line, puts the question. "There!" Hancock points to the gap by Cushing's guns, and the regiments of the brigade rush forward to throw themselves into the breach.[16]

From right and left the brigades of the Second

Corps press in. The two Pennsylvania regiments, which were pushed from the wall, have not fled, but have rallied behind the crest. Smyth's brigade is confronting Pettigrew, while Harrow's brigade comes from the left, and the Eighth Ohio, which has been on the picket line, closes in upon his flank. In the mêlée, uproar, confusion, and carnage, amid the roar of cannon, rolls of musketry, explosion of shells, whirring of canister and musket balls, amid yells and oaths and curses, brave deeds are done by Confederate and Union alike. There is an utter disregard of life — men in blue and men in gray are animated by one thought only — to conquer.

Fifteen minutes! It seems an hour. When General Pickett looks around for his supports they are not there to fold back the door which he has opened, and which has already closed again. The cannon of the cemetery have decimated the supporting brigades on the left, while Wilcox and Perry, who were to have come up on the right, are just starting from their positions west of the Emmitsburg Road, not to follow up his attack, but through some misdirection to make an independent and futile movement south of Codori's house.

The Confederates along the stone wall see that no help is at hand, that to attempt to retreat will be almost certain death, and four thousand five hundred throw down their arms and rush into the Union lines, while those farther out upon the field seek safety in flight. Then from Little

Round Top to Cemetery Hill rises a mighty chorus of voices shouting the paean of victory.

Says Longstreet, "When the smoke cleared away, Pickett's division was gone. Nearly two-thirds of his men lay dead on the field, and the survivors were sullenly retreating down the hill. In a half hour the contested field was cleared, and the Battle of Gettysburg was over."[17]

It was a feeble movement made by Wilcox and Perry — repulsed easily by McGilvery's guns — not made till too late to have any effect, for the battle had already been decided.

Lieutenant Colonel Freemantle, of the British army, was riding at the moment through the woods to Longstreet's position. This was his account:

"When I got close up to General Longstreet, I saw one of his regiments advancing through the woods in good order; so, thinking I was just in time to see the attack, I remarked to the general that 'I wouldn't have missed this for anything.' Longstreet was seated on the top of a snake fence, in the edge of the wood, and looking perfectly calm and unperturbed. He replied, 'The devil you wouldn't! I would like to have missed it very much; we've attacked and been repulsed. Look there!' "

"For the first time I then had a view of the open space between the two positions, and saw it covered with Confederates slowly and sulkily returning towards us in small broken parties. . . .

"I remember seeing a general (Pettigrew, I think it was) come up to him and report that he was unable to bring his men up again. Longstreet turned upon him and replied with some sarcasm, 'Very well, never mind, then, general; just let them remain where they are. The enemy is going to advance, and will spare you the trouble.' " . . .

"Soon afterwards I joined General Lee, who had in the mean while come to the front, on becoming aware of the disaster. He was engaged in rallying and in encouraging the troops. . . . He was addressing to every soldier he met a few words of encouragement, such as 'All this will come right in the end; we will talk it over afterwards, but in the mean time all good men must rally. We want all good men and true men just now,' etc. . . . He said to me, 'This has been a sad day for us, colonel, a sad day; but we can't expect always to gain victories.' . . . I saw General Wilcox (an officer who wears a short round jacket and a battered straw hat) come up to him, and explain, almost crying, the state of his brigade. General Lee immediately shook hands with him, and said, cheerfully, 'Never mind, general. All this has been my fault — it is I that have lost this fight, and you must help me out of it in the best way you can.' "[18]

The conflict had ceased in Codori's fields, but south of Round Top and out on Rummel's farm the cavalry were still engaged. The cavalry south of Round Top advanced resolutely, with two objects in view — the capture of some of Longstreet's trains, and a diversion which would prevent Longstreet from advancing once more against Little Round Top. Merritt's brigade deployed on the left, and attacked G. B. Anderson's Georgia Brigade, supported by two batteries. Farnsworth's brigade deployed on the right, next to Round Top, charged upon Backman's battery, and came near capturing it; but the Ninth Georgia Regiment, behind a stone wall, fired a volley by which Farnsworth was mortally wounded and his troops repulsed with much loss. It was cavalry attacking infantry, with the advantage pretty much on the side of the Confederates.

I had supposed the cavalry engagement ended when I rode back from the vicinity of Rummel's farm at one o'clock, but the great engagement between Stuart and Gregg did not begin till near the close of the cannonade preceding Pickett's charge. Stuart had placed himself in position to make the rout of the Union army complete, which it was confidently believed would be inaugurated by the assault of Hill's and Pickett's troops.

It was two o'clock when the First New Jersey Regiment advanced northward across a level field towards Mr. Rummel's house, to discover if any Confederates were in that direction, when out from Rummel's barn swarmed a strong body of dismounted Confederates, and the carbines began to rattle. A Confederate battery came galloping to the edge of the woods at the top of the hill north of Rummel's house, sending its shells across the field. Randol's Union battery replied.

There was brave fighting between men of the North and men of the South, Gregg holding his chosen ground and warding off every effort of Stuart. Union and Confederate alike could look across the intervening woodlands and see Cemetery Hill, Little Round Top, and the connecting ridge enveloped in smoke. They heard the rolls of musketry, and then the dying away of the battle. There was no rout of troops — no men in blue fleeing panic stricken down the Baltimore Turnpike. Possibly it nerved Stuart, and especially Hampton, to do something, if possible, to retrieve the waning fortune of the hour, for the charge of Hampton's brigade was bold and furious; but it was met and resisted. The sun was going down. The last blow had been struck, the Confederate troops fell back, and silence settled over all the scene. The Battle of Gettysburg had been fought and lost by General Lee. More than twenty thousand Confederates had been killed, wounded, or taken prisoners. The Union army had lost nearly as many.

Although the troops under Pickett had reached the ridge at one point, the entire Sixth Corps of the Union army, which had taken no part in the contest, together with the Third and Fifth Corps, were in position to fall upon them; and the supports which General Lee had arranged, even if the brigades had advanced with

Pickett, would have been cut to pieces. Longstreet, from his observation during the second day's engagement, had best comprehended the situation, and correctly judged that the movement would result in disaster.

It was a night of gloom and despondency in the Confederate army. During the three days' engagements nearly every regiment had taken part — the losses had been frightful. The Union army, which had been regarded with contempt, had defeated them. The confident expectation of victory which had inspired them all the way from Fredericksburg had suddenly given place to a consciousness that the great battle which they had counted on as a crowning victory had resulted in defeat. "These considerations made it to us one of those solemn and awful nights that any one who fought through our long war sometimes experienced before a great battle," are the words of a Confederate general.[19] The soldiers of both armies expected that with the rising sun the conflict would be renewed.

General Lee through the evening was turning over once more, as he never before had turned it, the great question of what to do. Fight another battle? Impossible; his ammunition was nearly gone. He must return to Virginia. With his large comprehension, in that hour of gloom it is not unlikely he saw that Gettysburg was the beginning of the end of the Confederacy. He was in consultation with A. P. Hill, examining maps by the flickering light of a candle. At one o'clock in the morning he came riding slowly to his own tent.

A Confederate officer, who had been directed to wait for him, has pictured the scene:

"There was not even a sentinel on duty, and no one of his staff was about. The moon was high in the heavens, shedding a flood of soft silvery light, almost as bright as day, upon the scene. When he approached and saw us, he spoke, reined in his horse, and essayed to dismount. The effort to do so betrayed so much physical exhaustion that I stepped forward to assist him, but before I reached him he had alighted. He threw his arm across the saddle to rest himself, and fixing his eyes upon the ground, leaned in silence upon his equally weary horse. The moon shone fully upon his massive features, and revealed an expression of sadness I had never seen upon that fine countenance before in any of the vicissitudes of the war through which he had passed. . . ."

" 'General, this has been a hard day on you.' "

This attracted his attention. He looked up, and replied, mournfully,

" 'Yes, it has been a sad, sad day to us,' " and immediately relapsed into his thoughtful mood and attitude. After a minute or two he suddenly straightened up to his full height, and turning to me with more animation, energy, and excitement of manner than I had ever seen in him before, addressed me in a voice tremulous with emotion, and said,

" 'General, I never saw troops behave more magnificently than Pickett's division of Virginians did today in their grand charge. And if they had been supported, as they were to have been, but for some reason not yet fully explained to me they were not, we would have held the position they so gloriously won at such a fearful loss of noble lives, and the day would have been ours.' After a moment he added, in a tone almost of agony, 'Too bad! *Too bad!* Too BAD!' "[20]

While yet the Confederates of Pickett's division who threw down their arms were rushing into the Union lines, I went down to the scene of the final conflict. Men in blue and men in gray, who had fired their muskets into one another's faces — so near that the powder had burned their clothing — were lying under the muzzles of Cushing's guns. The field between the stone wall and Codori's was very thickly strewn with prostrate forms — the dead of the second day's engagement, together with those that had gone down in the strife just ended. The wounded were calling for help, and already the hospital corps was upon the field, bringing Union and Confederate alike to the surgeons. Measure off a half mile in width, from Codori's to the crest of the ridge, extend the line south one mile to Rose's house and the wheat field, and you have a plot of ground on which, during the second and third day's engagement, more than fifteen thousand men were killed or wounded. Through the evening I surveyed the scene, walked amid the dead, beholding their faces in the moonlight — forms motionless evermore, life gone out. I thought of desolate homes North and South; of wife, mother, sister, or aged father, who would listen for footsteps which never would again be heard. Why such carnage of human life? Not personal hate; not obedience to autocrat or king, but the conflict between liberty and slavery, two eternally antagonistic, irreconcilable forms of society. Standing there, the conviction came that the slave power had wielded its mightiest blow; that when the remnants of Pickett's brigades drifted back across Codori's fields, it was the beginning of the ebb tide of the Confederacy.

It was nearly midnight when I rode up to General Meade's headquarters, in a grove east of the Taneytown Road. General Meade was sitting on a great flat boulder, listening to reports brought in by couriers. It was a scene which lives in memory. The evening breeze was gently rustling the green leaves over our heads; the katydids were singing cheerily. Around were bivouac fires, where soldiers were sitting, talking of the events of the day, and pointing to the trees shattered by cannon shot. Corps commanders were there, Howard, Sykes, Sedgwick, Pleasonton of the cavalry, Hunt of the artillery. General Meade had laid aside his slouched felt hat, that the breeze might fan his brow.

"Order up rations and ammunition," he said to his chief of staff.

"Let your limbers and caissons be refilled. Lee

may be up to something in the morning, and we must be ready for him," his words to General Hunt.

A band nearby struck up "Hail to the Chief," "Star Spangled Banner," and "Yankee Doodle." The soldiers listened and responded with a cheer.

The morning of July 4 dawned — anniversary of the Declaration of the Independence of the United States — the birth of the nation. From Cemetery Hill I could see with my glass the white canvas tops of army wagons and ambulances far away in the southwest moving towards the mountains. Were the Confederates retreating, or was it only the removal of the wounded? The Confederate pickets were still along the fields west of the Emmitsburg Road, exchanging shots with the Union videttes. The day passed with no aggressive movement by either army. Lee was improving the time sending his trains southward. Another day, and he had disappeared and was making his way to the Potomac. The Union army could not follow him with much hope of success, for in the mountain passes a brigade could hold a division at bay. General Meade lingered at Gettysburg when he should have been on the march. The cavalry under Kilpatrick and Gregg crossed the mountains, reached Hagerstown and Williamsport in advance of Stuart, fell upon a wagon train, captured several hundred prisoners, and burned the train. The pontoons which Lee had left at

Falling Waters had been destroyed on the second day of the battle by some Union cavalry sent by General French. Rain was falling, and the Potomac rising. Troops were hastening from all quarters to make good the losses of battle. The Union army marched cautiously. General Meade was undecided as to what he ought to do. General Lee reached the Potomac, where he received a supply of ammunition. His provisions were running low. He threw up entrenchments, collected canalboats, tore down houses, reconstructed a pontoon bridge, and when Meade, after much unaccountable delay, was ready to attack, the Confederate army was once more in Virginia. With the exception of Pettigrew's brigade, which Kilpatrick overtook at Falling Waters, the cavalrymen charged up a hill, with two cannon hurling canister in their faces, with muskets flashing, horses and men going down, but the men of Michigan in the saddle closed around the Confederates, cut off their retreat, and captured nearly nine hundred prisoners.

The invasion of the North was over; the great battle which was to bring about the independence of the Confederacy, its recognition as a nation by France and England, had been fought and lost.

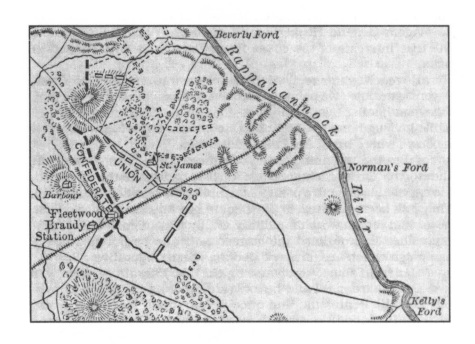

**BRANDY STATION, VIRGINIA**

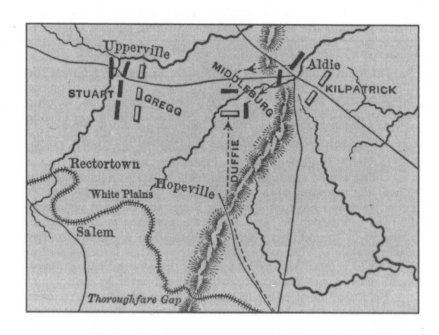

**CAVALRY ENGAGEMENTS AT ALDIE AND
UPPERVILLE, VIRGINIA**

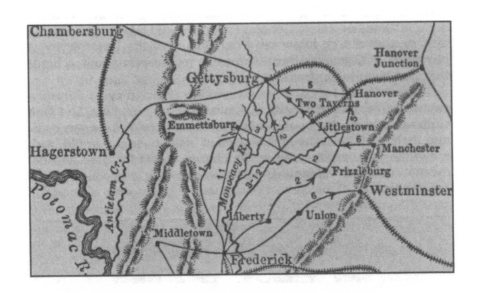

**MOVEMENT OF UNION ARMY TO
GETTYSBURG, PENNSYLVANIA**

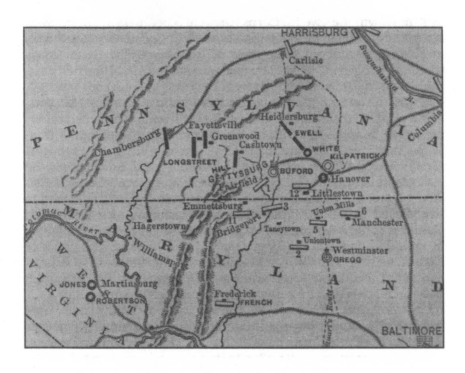

**POSITION OF UNION AND CONFEDERATE
ARMIES, SUNSET, JUNE 30, 1863**

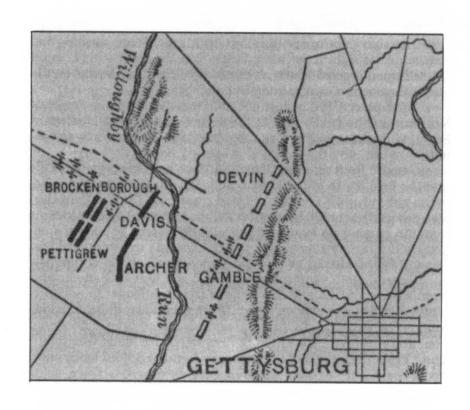

**OPENING OF BATTLE AT GETTYSBURG,
8 A.M., JULY 1, 1863**

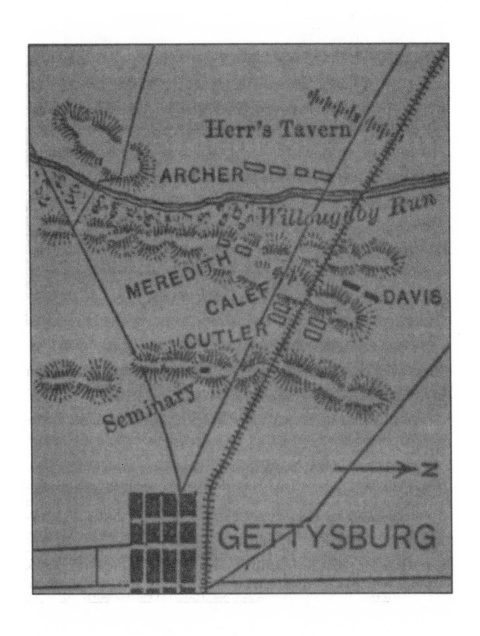

**BEGINNING OF INFANTRY ENGAGEMENT, 10 A.M., JULY 1, 1863**

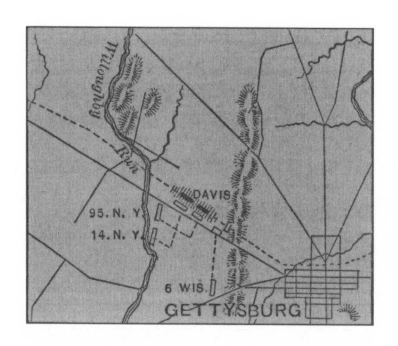

**CAPTURE OF CONFEDERATES IN THE RAILROAD AT GETTYSBURG**

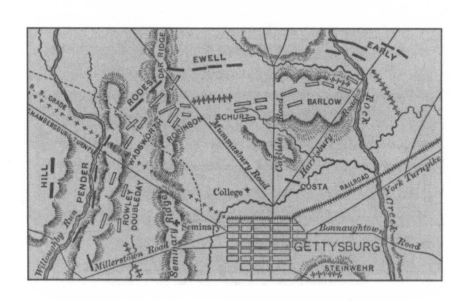

**FIRST DAY AT GETTYSBURG, AT 3 P.M.**

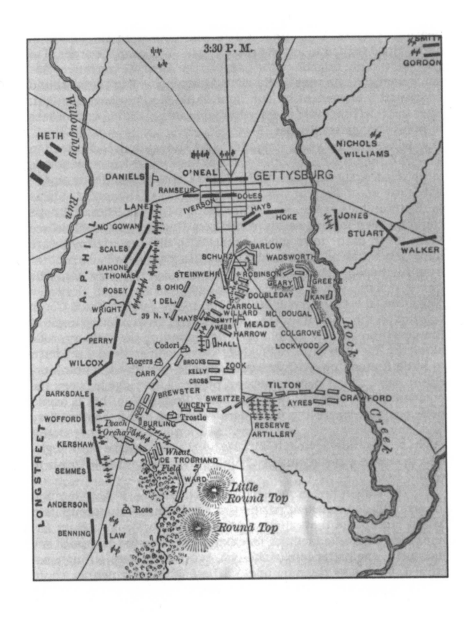

**POSITION OF UNION AND CONFEDERATE TROOPS, 3:30 P.M., JULY 2, 1863**

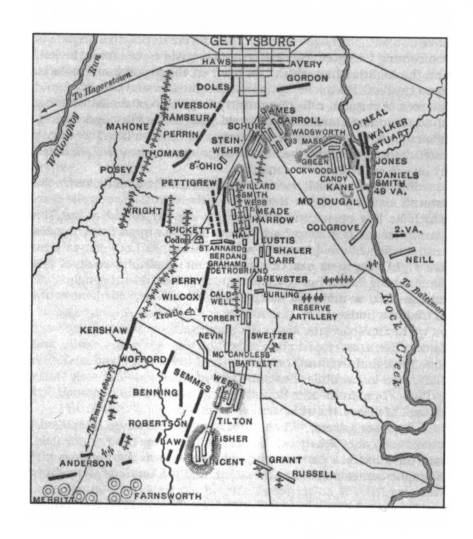

**POSITION OF TROOPS, THIRD DAY AT
GETTYSBURG**

190

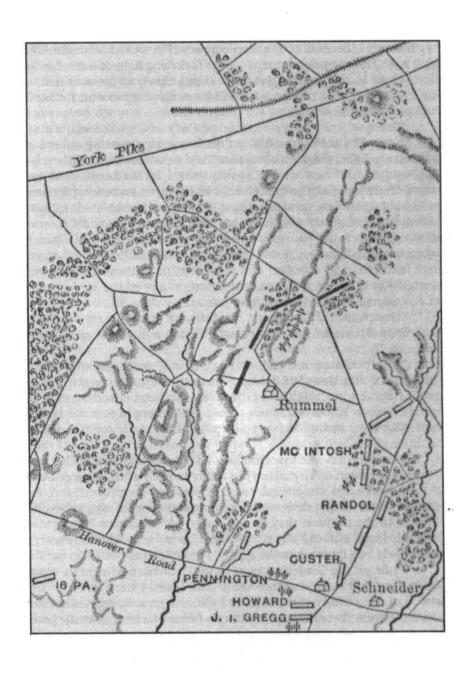

**CAVALRY ENGAGEMENT, THIRD DAY**

# Appendix A

## *Coffin's Course*

*Charles Coffin* arrived in Harrisburg, Pennsylvania, on June 15, 1863. There was great alarm because the Rebels were across the Potomac at Williamsport, Maryland. Many folks were fleeing from the Pennsylvania capital. Then, it was on to Baltimore where the residents were barricading streets and preparing to give the Confederates a warm welcome should they arrive at the gates of the city. Next stop, Frederick, Maryland. Coffin apparently arrived on Saturday and stayed at a hotel. It may have been the United States Hotel which was opposite the Baltimore and Ohio Railroad Station.

This seems most likely because the next morning Joseph Hooker gave his farewells to his staff amidst many tears. This was in the hotel lobby. After Gettysburg, Meade chose the United States Hotel as his temporary headquarters because of the close proximity to the train station and the telegraph.

In *The Boys of '61*, a synopsis of his Civil War coverage, Coffin says "I left the town (Frederick) accompanying the Second and Fifth

Corps. Long lines of men and innumerable wagons were visible in every direction. The people of Maryland welcomed the soldiers hospitably. . . ." This was the Second Corps commanded by Winfield Scott Hancock. In *Eyewitness to Gettysburg* he speaks on page seventy of meeting the infantry of the Fifth Corps in Liberty. The Fifth and the Second Corps took the same route to Liberty.

He continues by saying, "riding to Westminster I overtook General Gregg's division of cavalry, and on Wednesday moved forward to Hanover Junction which is thirty miles east of Gettysburg."

David M. Gregg commanded the Second Division of Cavalry, Army of the Potomac. Gregg's task, according to Pleasonton in the *Official Records* was "to move by the right flank of the army on Westminster, covering the country toward York and Carlisle by . . . patrols. On July 1, Gregg's Second Brigade commanded by Colonel Huey was at Hanover Junction (see page 110).

It was noon, July 1, 1863. The place, Hanover Junction. Coffin and others were feeding their horses corn. Suddenly they heard the sound of a great cannonade.

Smelling a story, Coffin quickly mounted and rode toward the sounds of the guns. However, he rode to Hanover. There he saw the debris of the cavalry engagement between Stuart and Kilpatrick. The wounded had been gathered into large public buildings, and the women of Hanover were treating them.

It was now evening, and the troops of the Fifth Corps had gone into bivouac. "Their campfires were gleaming in the meadows west of town, and the worn and weary soldiers were asleep, catching a few hours of repose before moving on to the place where they were to lay down their lives for their country."

Then it was on to Gettysburg traveling, what is now Route 116, through Bonneaghville. Coffin arrived at Little Round Top on July 2 (see page 116). En route he passed the infantry and their supply wagons. Coffin climbed the stairs at the cemetery gatehouse to observe the field.

He spoke with Oliver O. Howard and was impressed with the work of the courage of Josephine Miller as she baked bread in the presence of thousands of armed men. He had found Howard offering prayer for his food, and detailing soldiers to protect the gravestones in the cemetery.

He rode to Little Round Top and stood with an officer of the Signal Corps surveying the advance of Hood's troops (see page 132). Coffin was an eyewitness to the unfolding drama of July 2. He saw the deployment of Strong Vincent's brigade (see page 135).

On July 3, Coffin rode to Culp's Hill, thence to a point near East Cavalry field, and then back to Meade's headquarters. He was at the Leister house along the Taneytown Road when the

Confederate artillery bombardment began. He took cover with General Meade and his staff. Coffin was truly an eyewitness to Gettysburg.

# Appendix B

## *Personalities in Coffin's Account*

*These are* basically Union because Coffin rode with the Union army and saw the unfolding events while covering the infantry and cavalry of the Army of the Potomac.

John Buford, a native of Kentucky, and West Point class of 1848, had served in the west and then on the staff of John Pope. Later he was McClellan's chief of cavalry in the Maryland Campaign.

At Gettysburg, Buford fought for time, holding the high ground west of town until the infantry of the Army of the Potomac could assemble on the field. He ordered his men to hold McPherson's Ridge at all costs. Without his action, there may not have been a Gettysburg battle.

The rigors of the campaign, caused fatigue and illness. Buford was forced to take a sick leave. He expired in Washington on December 16, 1863, at the age of thirty-seven. His funeral service was attended by President Lincoln.

David M. Gregg graduated from West Point in 1855 and spent six years on the frontier fighting Indians. In 1861, Gregg was a captain in the Third U.S. Cavalry. During the Gettysburg Campaign, the Union cavalry was reorganized under the command of Alfred Pleasonton. The division commanders of the cavalry were John Buford, Judson Kilpatrick, and David McMurtrie Gregg.

In June, John Buford had the task of protecting the left flank of the Army of the Potomac. Kilpatrick moved with army headquarters on what is now Maryland Route 194, while Gregg moved by the right flank of the army and thence toward Gettysburg. Coffin was with Gregg at Hanover Junction on July 1 when he received the news of the encounter at Gettysburg.

Winfield Scott Hancock, known as "Hancock the Superb," was without equal as a corps commander. The native of Norristown, Pennsylvania, played a pivotal role on each day at Gettysburg. On July 1, he stabilized the Union line on Cemetery Ridge; on July 2, he sent troops to repulse Confederate forces attacking up the Emmitsburg Road; and on July 3, Hancock's Second Corps repulsed Pickett's charge. Coffin was in the rear of Hancock's lines during the Confederate attack. Hancock advocated humane treatment for the South after the war, and narrowly lost the 1880 presidential election to James Garfield.

Ambrose Powell Hill of Culpeper, Virginia,

and a member of the famed class of 1846, had also been the roommate of George B. McClellan while at the academy. At the outbreak of the war he rose rapidly in rank, and had no equal as a commander of the light division. His rapid march from Harpers Ferry to Sharpsburg saved the Army of Northern Virginia on September 17, 1862.

With the death of Jackson, Hill was given command of the newly created Third Corps. At Gettysburg, and in other engagements, he seemed out of his league as a corps commander.

With his reddish beard and red battle shirt, Hill cut a dashing figure. He was killed just before the end of the war near Petersburg.

Oliver O. Howard, from Maine, and West Point class of 1854, had lost his right arm at Fair Oaks. He led a division in the Second Corps at Antietam and at Fredericksburg. He commanded the Eleventh Corps at Chancellorsville and Gettysburg. After the war, he did much to help the blacks and founded Howard University in Washington. Howard was also superintendent at West Point. He was active in religious and educational projects.

George Gordon Meade was rudely awakened in the early morning hours of Sunday, June 28, 1863. He had gone to sleep at Arcadia on the Buckeystown Pike, now Route 85, as commander of the Union Fifth Corps. Colonel Hardie brought orders for a new assignment, commander of the Army of the Potomac. Meade must be commended for the task he did on the eve of the battle, bringing the army together on Cemetery Ridge and directing the battle. He was criticized for not pursuing Lee more vigoriously after Gettysburg. However, he was chasing a wounded foe, and the Army of the Potomac had suffered 23,000 casualties, including many key officers. Meade remained with the Army of the Potomac until the end of the war.

Patrick H. O'Rorke was a young colonel from Rochester, New York. He had graduated at the head of the West Point class of 1861, and assumed command of the 140th New York. He was beloved by officers and men alike. O'Rorke was called upon to protect and defend Little Round Top. The young officer was one of the many in the brigade who gave "his last full measure of devotion" on Little Round Top.

John Fulton Reynolds, the former commandant of cadets at West Point, led the left wing of the Union Army, on the roads to Gettysburg, directing the First, Third, and Eleventh Corps. Offered command of the army a month earlier, Reynolds had declined the offer. Meade had placed Reynolds in a position of great trust.

Reynolds was killed near McPherson's Ridge in mid-morning on July 1, not far from his Lancaster, Pennsylvania home. In his death, the Republic lost a great officer and a gentleman.

Daniel E. Sickles, the egotistical, flamboyant commander of the Union Third Corps, remains the center of controversy whenever scholars debate the actions of the second day at Gettysburg, and the movement to the Peach Orchard. Some say, Sickles nearly lost the battle, while others are of the opinion that his actions were positive. Sickles lost his leg near the Trostle farm. The stump was saved, and whenever Sickles returned to Gettysburg for reunions, he went to the museum, obtained his amputated leg and took it with him to Gettysburg.

John Sedgwick, from Cornwall Hollow, Connecticut and a graduate of the West Point class of 1837, was affectionately known to his command as "Uncle John." Prior to the Civil War, he had served as a major in the First U.S. Cavalry. The commanding officer of the unit was Colonel Robert E. Lee.

Badly wounded at Antietam, Sedgwick returned to the Army of the Potomac to lead the Sixth Corps on the roads to Gettysburg. On June 29–30, he was on the far right of the Union line and camped at Manchester, Maryland.

About 9 P.M. on July 1, he was ordered to Gettysburg. His command made an epic thirty-four mile march in approximately eighteen hours to reinforce the Army of the Potomac on Cemetery Ridge.

Sedgwick was killed in action the following spring.

George Sykes, the officer who assumed command of the Fifth Corps when Meade was promoted to army command, was born in Dover, Delaware, on October 22, 1822. Graduating from West Point, he was part of the class that gave twelve army and corps commanders to the Union and Confederate cause. At First Bull Run, he commanded elements of the Fourteenth Infantry which covered the Union retreat. Coffin rode with Sykes and the Fifth Corps from Hanover to Gettysburg. After the war, Sykes commanded the Twentieth Infantry in Texas and Minnesota. He died in 1880 and is buried at West Point.

Strong Vincent, a Harvard graduate, had made the Eighty-third Pennsylvania Infantry, one of the superior regiments in the Fifth Corps. His first name was indicative of courage and character. On the roads to Gettysburg, although a colonel, he was acting brigade commander, and also observed his twenty-sixth birthday. Somewhere near Hanover, he watched the regimental flag being unfurled, and said, "What death more glorious can any man desire, than to die on the soil of old Pennsylvania fighting for that flag." Little did he know that in a few more hours, he would have a rendezvous with destiny and death, as his unit arrived just in time to save Little Round Top. A monument in his honor stands on the southern slope he fought and died to defend.

# Appendix C

## *Places in Coffin's Course*

*Frederick, like* Gettysburg, was the hub of a road and rail network. Thus the Army of the Potomac made the city its objective as it sought to remain between Lee's army and the large eastern cities. With the exception of the Union Sixth Corps, the rest of the Army of the Potomac marched through Frederick on June 28 and 29. Frederick had a population of 8,000 during the Civil War. Frederick also became the Union base of operations after Gettysburg.

Hanover, Pennsylvania, named after the German city by the same name, witnessed the encounter of Judson Kilpatrick's cavalry with that of Jeb Staurt on June 30. One of the leading participants in the action was the boy general, George A. Custer. Coffin rode through Hanover on July 1 heading for Gettysburg.

Liberty, this quaint town east of Frederick, on current Maryland Route 26, witnessed the approach march of the Union Fifth and Second Corps on the roads to Gettysburg. Apparently the town derived its name from the Sons of Liberty organization. Coffin rode from Frederick on

Monday, June 29, to ride with the Fifth Corps the rest of the day.

Westminster is the seat of government for Carroll County, Maryland. It was in this town that Coffin began riding with David Gregg's cavalry division. Westminster was designated at the main supply depot for the Army of the Potomac after the troops had crossed the Mason Dixon Line. Trains also transported the wounded and prisoners of the Battle of Gettysburg through Westminster to Baltimore.

# *Notes*

## Chapter I

1. *Richmond Examiner*, May 21, 1863.
2. James Longstreet, "Annals of the War," p. 416.
3. *Richmond Examiner*, May 30, 1863.
4. Hotze to Judah Benjamin, August 4, 1863.
5. Hotze to Benjamin, June 6, 1863.
6. George Mason to Benjamin, March 31, 1863.
7. Slidell to Benjamin, June 18, 1863.
8. Slidell to Benjamin, June 25, 1863.
9. Coffin's interviews with Confederate soldiers.
10. *Richmond Examiner*, June 12, 1863.

## Chapter II

1. W. B. McClellan, "Life and Campaigns of Major General J. E. B. Stuart," Boston, 1885, p. 316.
2. General Robert E. Lee's Letter of June

23, 1863.

3. Jacob Hoke, "The Great Invasion," Chambersburg, 1887, p. 143.
4. Ibid., p. 162.
5. Ibid., p. 164.
6. McClellan, "Life and Campaigns of Stuart," p. 322.
7. J. L. Snesseratt, "Great Invasion," p. 205.
8. General Robert E. Lee in *War of the Rebellion: A Compilation of the Official Records of the Union and Confederate Armies*, vol. 27, pts. 1, 2 and 3 deal with Gettysburg, p. 293. Hereafter cited as *OR*.
9. Longstreet, "Annals of the War," part 1, pp. 293, 419.
10. Ibid.
11. General Henry Hunt, *Century Magazine*, November 1886.
12. London *Times*, July 1, 1863.

# Chapter III

1. General John Buford's Report, *OR*, p. 921.
2. General Henry Heth's Report, *OR*, p. 921.
3. General Gamble's Report, *OR*, p. 933.
4. Lieutenant Calef's Report, *OR*, p. 1030.
5. Captain Bronson's Statement, unpublished papers (War Department).

6. J. V. Pierce, One Hundred and Forty-seventh New York Regiment, *National Tribune.*
7. Captain Hall's Report.
8. G. C. Kimball's Memorial Address, Thirteenth Massachusetts Regiment.
9. Colonel Hoffman to Governor Curtin.
10. General Wadsworth's Report, *OR*, p. 286.
11. General Fairchild's Report, *OR*, p. 273.
12. General Abner Doubleday, "Chancellorsville and Gettysburg," p. 130.
13. *Century Magazine*, November 1886, p. 106.
14. Lieutenant Colonel Dudley, unpublished papers (War Department).
15. Captain Hall's Statement, unpublished papers (War Department).
16. Lieutenant Colonel Rufus Dawes's Statement, unpublished papers (War Department).
17. General Howard to author.
18. Longstreet, "Annals of the War," p. 420.
19. General Oliver Howard's Report.
20. General Iverson's Report.
21. General Rodes's Report.
22. General Howard's Report.
23. Samuel Wilkeson to author.
24. General A. P. Hill's Report.
25. Mr. Shead to author.
26. General Howard to author, July 2, 1863.
27. Longstreet, "Annals of the War," p. 421.
28. Ibid.
29. Longstreet, *Century Magazine*, February 1887.

# Chapter IV

1. Longstreet, "Annals of the War," p. 422.
2. Longstreet, *Century Magazine*, February 1887.
3. Josephine Miller to author.
4. Longstreet, "Annals of the War," p. 422.
5. Berdan, Statement, *National Tribune*, 1886.
6. Owen, "In Camp and Battle," p. 244.
7. General Evander Law, *Century Magazine*, December 1886.
8. General Henry Hunt, *Century Magazine*, December 1886.
9. Colonel Sheffield, unpublished papers (War Department).
10. Colonel Perry, unpublished papers (War Department).
11. "Story of a Boy's Company," p. 139.
12. General Warren to Porter Farley, *Rochester Democrat*, December 3, 1877.
13. Porter Farley, *Rochester Democrat*, December 3, 1877.
14. General McLaws to J. W. Baker, "History of the Ninth Massachusetts Battery."
15. Major Bigelow, "History of the Ninth Massachusetts Battery."
16. Ibid.
17. Colonel Herbert, Eighth Alabama, unpublished papers (War Department).
18. General Francis Walker, "History of the Second Corps," p. 283.

19. McGinnis, Memorial Address, before First Minnesota Regiment.

## Chapter V

1. General Longstreet, "Annals of the War," p. 427.
2. Captain Harwood, "Virginia Fifty-third."
3. Colonel E. P. Alexander, *Century Magazine*, January 1887.
4. General Henry Hunt, *Century Magazine*, January 1887.
5. General Longstreet, "Annals of the War," p. 431.
6. Colonel E. P. Alexander, *Century Magazine*, January 1887.
7. Captain Owen, "In Camp and Battle," p. 253.
8. Colonel E. P. Alexander, *Century Magazine*, January 1887.
9. General Longstreet, "Annals of the War," p. 430.
10. Colonel E. P. Alexander, *Century Magazine*, January 1887.
11. General Howard and Major Osborn to author.
12. Captain Harwood, "Virginia Fifty-third."
13. Captain Owen, "In Camp and Battle," p. 251.
14. Captain Harwood, "Virginia Fifty-third."
15. General Stannard to author.
16. Hancock's account.

17. General Longstreet, "Annals of the War," p. 431.
18. *Blackwood's Magazine*, September 1863.
19. General John Imboden, *Galaxy Magazine*, April 1871.
20. Ibid.

# *Bibliography*

For additional reading on the inspiring events witnessed and written about Charles C. Coffin, we refer you to other sources:

## Overview

Coddington, Edwin B. *The Gettysburg Campaign*. New York: Scribners, 1968.

## The Approach March

Hoke, Jacob. *The Great Invasion*. New York, 1959. Like Coffin, Hoke, living in Franklin County, Pennsylvania, was an eyewitness to the events.

Schildt, John W. *Roads to Gettysburg*. Parsons, W.Va.: McClain Press, 1978.

## The First Day

Hassler, Warren W. *No Crises at the Crossroads*. University of Alabama Press, 1970.

# The Second Day

Pfanz, Harry W. *Gettysburg: The Second Day.* Chapel Hill: The University of North Carolina Press, 1987.